# THE CAMBRIDGE HISTORY OF
# CLASSICAL LITERATURE

GENERAL EDITORS
Mrs P. E. Easterling *Fellow of Newnham College, Cambridge*
E. J. Kenney *Fellow of Peterhouse, Cambridge*

ADVISORY EDITORS
B. M. W. Knox *The Center for Hellenic Studies, Washington*
W. V. Clausen *Department of the Classics, Harvard University*

# VOLUME II PART 5
# THE LATER PRINCIPATE

# THE CAMBRIDGE HISTORY OF
# CLASSICAL LITERATURE

## VOLUME II: LATIN LITERATURE

# THE CAMBRIDGE HISTORY OF CLASSICAL LITERATURE

## VOLUME II

### PART 5

## The Later Principate

EDITED BY

### E. J. KENNEY
*Fellow of Peterhouse, Cambridge*

ADVISORY EDITOR

### W. V. CLAUSEN
*Professor of Greek and Latin*
*Harvard University*

## CAMBRIDGE UNIVERSITY PRESS

CAMBRIDGE
LONDON   NEW YORK   NEW ROCHELLE
MELBOURNE   SYDNEY

Published by the Press Syndicate of the University of Cambridge
The Pitt Building, Trumpington Street, Cambridge CB2 1RP
32 East 57th Street, New York, NY 10022, USA
296 Beaconsfield Parade, Middle Park, Melbourne 3206, Australia

First published 1982 as chapters 35–42 and Epilogue of *The Cambridge History
of Classical Literature*, Volume II
First paperback edition 1983

Printed in Great Britain by the University Press, Cambridge

Library of Congress catalogue card number: 82-19784

*British Library Cataloguing in Publication Data*

The Cambridge history of classical literature.
Vol. 2: Latin literature
The Later principate
1. Classical literature – History and criticism
I. Kenney, E. J. II. Clausen, W. V.
880'.09 PA3001
ISBN 0 521 27371 4

# CONTENTS

# CONTENTS

# 1

## INTRODUCTORY

The period to be studied in this chapter extends roughly from the middle of the third century to the middle of the fifth century A.D. Looked at from the point of view of the history of the Roman Empire it can be divided into several stages. The first extends from the death of Alexander Severus in 235 to the proclamation of Diocletian as emperor in 284. This was a half-century of chaos and disorder throughout the empire. The delicate balance of political power broke down, and legitimacy was no longer conferred upon emperors by a consensus, however formal, of Senate, people and army, and sustained by the general consent of the ruling classes of the cities in both east and west. Local interest groups began to proclaim their own candidates for imperial power. The most effective of these were the provincial armies and to a lesser degree the Praetorian Guard at Rome. The half-century of disorder was begun by the assassination of Alexander Severus at Moguntiacum (Mainz) and the proclamation by the army there of Maximinus, a Thracian officer who had risen from the ranks. Soon the influential land-owning class of Africa proclaimed their candidate, Gordian. The powerless Senate vacillated between the two claimants and for a time put forward its own candidates, Balbinus and Pupienus. And so it went on. The situation was one of almost permanent civil war, marked not only by several pitched battles between Roman armies, but also by a break-down of civil administration and legality and the growth of arbitrary rule by military commanders, who could maintain their armies in being only by letting them live directly on the produce of the citizens they were supposed to defend. Rarely throughout the half-century were there not several claimants to imperial power in the field at once, each striving to exercise the civil and military authority of a *princeps* without enjoying the support upon which that authority was based. More and more effective, even if short-lived, power passed into the hands of a class which had enjoyed little esteem or influence in the heyday of the Empire, namely the military men from the frontier provinces. This does not mean, as some of our sources suggest and as some modern scholars have believed, that power passed into the hands of peasant soldiers. The officers who aspired to imperial authority and their entourages were rather men from the small towns which had grown up near legionary headquarters along the Rhine and Danube, and often persons of some substance. But they had not hitherto enjoyed the direct or indirect influence upon decisions which belonged to the senatorial order and to the urban upper classes of the Mediterranean provinces. What they gained in power the older ruling classes lost.

At the same time as this breakdown of the old power structure, the ring of military defences which surrounded the empire began to be more frequently and more seriously breached. It would be hard to say which was cause and which effect. The Alemanni and Franks invaded Gaul and Rhaetia again and again. Goths, Carpi, Vandals, Taifali and other east Germanic peoples swept southwards through Moesia and Thrace year after year. In 267 they captured and pillaged Corinth, Argos and Athens. Dacia was submerged under a barbarian tide and lost for ever to the empire. On the eastern frontier a renascent Persia under a new dynasty challenged Rome. In 256 Antioch fell to the Persians, who installed a puppet emperor there. In 260 the emperor Valerian was taken prisoner by a Persian army, which went on to invade Cilicia and Cappadocia. Further south the client kingdom of Palmyra profited by Roman weakness to extend its sway as far as Egypt in the south and Antioch and Cilicia in the north. Not unnaturally this succession of calamities was accompanied by rapid debasement of the currency and raging inflation. This was a half-century during which those social groups which had provided both patronage and readership for literature were in disarray, and the occasions for public display of literary skill were few. Little remains of Latin writing from the period, and little seems to have been written of any value. But one must not exaggerate the sharpness of the break. Urban life and culture were much less threatened in the Greek east than in the Latin west, in spite of the aggressive policies of Persia and Palmyra. And in the more disturbed west Plotinus continued giving lectures on philosophy to his distinguished and influential audience in Rome from 244 to 269 without apparently suffering any interruption. But Rome was no longer at the centre of power.

The next period, that of Diocletian (284–305) and Constantine (307–37) saw the re-establishment of firm central power in the empire on a new basis. Diocletian inaugurated a system of collegiate imperial power, with two senior and two junior emperors, who derived their legitimacy from a supposed divine selection and protection. A radical restructuring of imperial administration was undertaken, in which the number of provinces was increased, the senatorial order was excluded from holding military command, and a new concentration of power appeared in the much enlarged imperial court, which no longer resided at Rome but moved from province to province in the frontier regions as the military situation demanded. This arrangement institutionalized the accession to power of a new class from the frontier provinces which did not entirely share Italian traditions and ideals.

Constantine, after a series of confrontations with co-emperors and rivals, abandoned the system of collegiate power and ruled from 324 to 337 as sole emperor. He completed the work of reorganization of Diocletian, re-established the currency on a firm basis, founded a new second capital city at Byzantium on the Bosphorus, and began to draw into the circle of power once again, although only to a limited degree, the Italian senatorial class. He also sought support from a group in Roman society which hitherto had been unconcerned with or actually excluded from power. The Christian religion was first tolerated and later preferred and patronized by Constantine, who sought in it a source of legitimation of his own authority. The church, though still comprising only a minority of the subjects of the empire, gained rapidly in prestige, influence and wealth. Bishops formed a part of Constantine's court entourage. The urban upper classes began to embrace the new religion in greater numbers and to bring with them into the Christian milieu many of the attitudes and values of traditional classical culture.

By Constantine's death stability had been restored in the military, administrative and economic spheres. Literature and art began to find patrons once again, and the pen began to replace the sword as an instrument of persuasion. The last two thirds of the fourth century were not without civil wars and disturbances. But on the whole they were an age of steady government and of relative prosperity. Literature flourished more fruitfully than it had since the days of the Antonines. But it was a literature changed both in form and in content. Some genres were no longer practised. There was no epic poetry, no drama, no forensic or political oratory. Others, as will be seen, extended their range. As the Christians increased in numbers and influence, overtly Christian writing formed an ever larger part of Latin literature. This falls into several categories. Writing by Christians on classical or at any rate not specifically Christian themes will be treated in the following pages in exactly the same way as pagan writings. Works written by Christians on Christian topics for Christian readers will generally not be discussed. This category comprises dogmatic and homiletic writing, works dealing with ecclesiastical organization and discipline, sectarian polemic, pastoral treatises, and the like. There remains a considerable body of literature on Christian topics addressed expressly to non-Christians and of Christian works couched in more or less strictly classical form, and hence likely to be read and appreciated by the classically educated. This literature will be discussed briefly in the light of its place in classical literary tradition, but there will be no systematic treatment of its place in the development of Christian thought in the Latin west. Needless to say, none of these categories is demarcated with unequivocal clarity. There are grey areas around all of them.

The final period, in the first half of the fifth century, saw the political separation between the eastern and western parts of the empire, which had been a temporary expedient in the past, become permanent. From being temporary invaders or mercenary forces, Germanic peoples from beyond the frontier became permanent settlers in the empire, and often set up their own governments in the territories which they occupied. In 410 the Visigoths captured Rome, an event whose effect upon the imagination of contemporaries it would be impossible to exaggerate. Visigoths and Burgundians established themselves permanently in southern Gaul, setting up there what were in effect independent kingdoms. Parts of the Iberian peninsula were similarly occupied by Visigoths and Suebi. Towards the middle of the century the Vandals, after sweeping through Spain, crossed the straits of Gibraltar and by 439 were in control of the rich and populous province of Africa and its capital city Carthage. Their power soon extended to Sardinia and Corsica, and by 455 a Vandal force captured and pillaged Rome itself, causing far greater damage to life and property than the Visigoths had done. During this period Christianity became not merely the predominant but virtually the sole religion of the empire. A synthesis of classical and Christian culture began to be formed in the west, which was distinct from that of the Greek east. The church and its hierarchy took over some of the functions and the prestige which had hitherto belonged to officials of the state, and cultural leadership began to pass to bishops, who themselves were often the sons or grandsons of pagan men of literary distinction. The whole social framework within which classical literature had been written, read and criticized was unmistakably changed. It is symptomatic that a great landed proprietor and senator who had written panegyrics upon emperors replete with classical allusions and motives ended his days as a Christian bishop in a Germanic kingdom.

Certain general features of the life and literature of late antiquity call for brief discussion at this point as part of the background to the study of particular writers and their works. They will all find illustration and exemplification in the pages which follow this general introduction. The first is the loosening of the cultural unity of the upper classes of the empire, and in particular of the bonds between the Greek east and the Latin west. They had always been conscious, and indeed proud, of the differences which separated them. Yet the Greek sophists of the second century had moved easily between Ephesus or Pergamum and Rome. Aelius Aristides had given eloquent expression to his consciousness of belonging to a Roman society which embraced and transcended the world of Greek culture. Greeks like Appian, Cassius Dio and Herodian wrote on Roman history. A Roman emperor wrote his diary not only in the Greek language but in terms of Greek philosophical concepts. During the fifty years of anarchy the Greek east suffered much less than the Latin west. The Latin world was to some extent left to its own resources, and knowledge of the Greek language, Greek literature and Greek thought became much rarer in the west than it had been in the previous three centuries. This break in contact did not begin to be healed until the late fourth century. Even a man like Augustine – Manichaean, Neoplatonist, rhetorician and Christian philosopher – was not at his ease in Greek, and the intellectual leaders of the Roman aristocracy often had only a school-room knowledge of the language. Towards the end of the century a new strengthening of contact began. Several leading Latin writers were actually Greeks by birth and culture. The Gaulish aristocracy of the early fifth century were often familiar with Greek literature and thought, their Italian counterparts on the whole less so. But the old sense of unity was never restored. Greek and Latin remained separate, their relations often having a diplomatic or missionary character. Latin literature ceased to draw continuously upon Greek sources and Greek models, as it had done since the days of Ennius, and became more self-contained. The sharpness of the cultural break must not be exaggerated. There were always men in the west who knew and read Greek. But they were fewer in number and in influence than in the great days of the Roman Empire. This is as true of Christians as of pagans, perhaps even truer, in spite of the ecumenical nature of the Christian church. In the fourth and fifth centuries Christian thought and expression struck a different tone in Latin and in Greek. The Cappadocian Fathers Gregory of Nyssa, Basil and Gregory of Nazianzus, and their younger contemporary John Chrysostom were little known to western Christians, Ambrose and Augustine were totally unknown in the east. Men like Jerome and Rufinus tried to build a bridge between the two halves of the Christian world by their translations and adaptations, but met with only limited success.

A second feature of the period which has significant effects on Latin literature is the 'depoliticization' – if such a word is permissible – of the Roman senatorial class. Excluded in the half-century of anarchy from participation in the exercise of state power, and only partially and grudgingly re-admitted to a limited group of public offices in the fourth century, the senatorial order retained its immense landed wealth and much of its social prestige. As patrons, writers and readers of literature the senatorial class tended to adopt a backward-looking, antiquarian stance, reflecting its disengagement from contemporary affairs. Idealization of an imagined past and obsessive concentration upon traditional forms became almost the symbols of status. The grammarian, the lexicographer, the antiquarian and the commentator took the place of the original and creative writer. Instead of writing the history of their own times, in which they often had little interest, senators of literary inclination would prepare – or have prepared for them by others – luxurious manuscripts of Livy or Virgil or Sallust. The distinction between school and real life became blurred. There is often a curiously juvenile quality in the literature of late antiquity. A similar development can be seen in the Greek east too. But it was much less marked and its social basis was less clear. For in the east there was no class corresponding to the senatorial order of the west, rich, long-established, sure of its local authority and accustomed to participate in the affairs of the empire. This 'disengagement' of the senatorial class is a peculiarly western phenomenon.

A further feature, connected in part with the changed position of the Roman senatorial order, is the development of centres of literature outside Rome itself. The removal of the court from Rome to Milan, Trier, Sirmium, Constantinople, Nicomedia or Antioch meant that a new centre of imperial patronage existed. The provincialization of the senatorial order, and the citizenship of all free men, contributed to creating the conditions for a Latin literature less exclusively Rome-centred than in the past. Africa had already established a more locally based Latin literature, though many African writers, like Fronto, lived and wrote in Rome. Christian writers, from Tertullian onwards, were often closely concerned with the problems of the provincial society of which they were members. For all these, and no doubt other less readily identifiable reasons the Latin literature, both pagan and Christian, of late antiquity has to some extent broken with Rome. Ausonius writes in Bordeaux and at Trier, Claudian's poems are recited in Milan. Sidonius Apollinaris' life and work are centred on his native Auvergne. Augustine writes largely in Africa and often for an African readership, Juvencus composes his poem in Spain, Rufinus writes most of his works in Aquileia, Jerome in Bethlehem. Latin literature is no longer necessarily Roman literature.

The growth of a 'committed' literature within the expanding Christian community is a topic which largely falls outside the scope of the present study. But the entanglement of Christian–pagan polemic with the antiquarian frondism of the Roman senatorial order in the second half of the fourth century lent a sharp edge to controversy and made the confrontation between Christianity and paganism take a somewhat different course, in literary terms, in the Latin west from that which it followed in the Greek east. For a time the conflict of religions threatened to become a conflict of cultures, in which the whole classical Roman tradition was set against a new Christian culture which expressly rejected much of the pagan past. Jerome's famous dream, in which he saw himself accused of being a Ciceronian rather than a Christian (*Epist.* 22.20) has no parallel in the east, nor has the bitter but dignified polemic

6

between Ambrose and Symmachus over the altar of Victory in the senate-house. Roman society and Latin literature surmounted this conflict, and a viable synthesis of classical and Christian tradition was in the end attained. But it never had the easy and unstrained character of Christian classicism in the Greek east. There was no Latin equivalent of Basil's address to the young on how to read profane literature.

There is another general characteristic of literature and art, and indeed of all aspects of public life, in late antiquity which is hard to define, but whose reality is clear enough to all students of the period. Public deportment acquires a theatrical character, public utterance a tone of declamatory exaggeration. At the imperial court an elaborate ceremonial serves to isolate an emperor whose public appearances, carefully stage-managed, have something of the character of a theophany. Men admired Constantius II on his visit to Rome, recounts a contemporary historian, because he held himself immobile in his carriage, his eyes raised to heaven, looking neither to left nor to right. The same emperor is depicted on a silver dish from Kerch, now in the Hermitage at Leningrad, seated on his horse, larger than the other human figures, a nimbus round his head, gazing through the spectator with huge, wide-open eyes. The sculptured head of Constantine in the Palazzo dei Conservatori at Rome and the colossal statue of an unknown emperor at Barletta show this same hieratic remoteness from ordinary people and everyday life. In the missorium of Theodosius, now in the Academía de la Historia, Madrid, the emperor, nimbate and of super-human stature, wearing a jewelled diadem and a large jewelled clasp, stares into space with the same unnaturally large eyes. Examples could be multiplied indefinitely. Court officials and provincial governors affected the same style, no longer walking through the streets but travelling in ornate carriages accompanied by guards of honour. Modes of address became more complex and honorific. An emperor spoke of himself as *serenitas nostra* and addressed a Prefect of the City as *tua celsitudo*. Even Symmachus, the champion of ancient senatorial usage, addresses his friend Ausonius in a letter as *unanimitas tua*. Laws, proclamations, and official correspondence of all kinds are couched in an inflated, circumlocutory, repetitious style with a plethora of abstract expressions. This is as true of Greek as of Latin, and applies with equal force to the decrees of an emperor and the letters of a minor tax official in Egypt. Often the tone of such a document, with its repeated – and vague – protestations and threats, suggests to the modern reader that the writer was on the verge of hysteria. Naturally not all literature is equally affected by this tendency to overstatement. But even those who swim against the tide are carried with it. Everywhere the restraint and reserve which marked much of classical culture give way to a more strident and declamatory tone.

7

All these factors, and no doubt many others which we cannot so clearly discern, led in late antiquity to an effacement of the traditional distinctions between literary genres. Panegyric – and its opposite, invective – are composed in the metre and language of epic poetry. Didactic poems are written in elegiac couplets. The tale of the Trojan war is retold in flat, uniform prose. The letter is used for public polemic. The principles of Christian dogma are set forth in Horatian lyrics. Satire as such is no longer written. But the satirical manner colours many other kinds of writing, such as Arnobius' refutations of pagan doctrines, Claudian's political lampoons, many of Jerome's letters on moral and theological themes. New genres begin to emerge, as writers seek an appropriate literary form for new kinds of content. An example is the kind of autobiography in which the writer reveals something of his inner life. Augustine writes his in highly rhetorical prose. Paulinus of Nola chooses traditional hexameter verse, but without all the apparatus of classical allusion which traditionally belonged to it. In a period in which traditional rules no longer held there was naturally much formless, rambling writing, both in prose and in verse. But it would be a mistake to suppose that the chief characteristic of late Latin literature is decadence. The period saw the development of new literary forms and new techniques. Among the most important of these, judged by its consequences, is the sustained allegory, first developed by Prudentius in verse and by Martianus Capella in prose. Augustine was in many respects a most unclassical writer. But that he wrote powerfully and compellingly cannot be denied. Claudian uses the metre and language of epic poetry for strange purposes. But he uses them strikingly and effectively. The literature of late antiquity combined tradition and innovation, and often in a truly creative fashion.

Finally, the gradual, non-revolutionary character of the changes in life and literature must be emphasized. Two hundred years is a long time. It would be a great mistake to suppose that late antique man was as aware that he was living in an epoch of radical and irreversible change as we are today. Nothing was sudden. The old persisted along with the new. Much continued apparently unchanged. Among the literate the sense of continuity was sustained by a highly traditional system of education based on the detailed study of a small number of classical texts. No one, not even the most innovatory of new men in power, thought for a moment of changing this system. Constantine confirmed the privileges of professors. More than two centuries later, after Italy had been devastated by twenty years of war, Justinian restored the emoluments and privileges of teachers of rhetoric. Everything conspired to create the illusion of immutability, and innovators could only conceive of their own measures as acts of restoration. From none of the epitomizing historians of late antiquity would the casual reader gain the impression that the fourth century was in any significant way different from the centuries that preceded. Only Ammianus Marcellinus had the insight to perceive that he was living and writing in an age of crisis, though he never attempts to define the nature of the crisis. Christian writers, with their essentially historical view of the world, were sometimes more sensitive to the signs of change than their pagan contemporaries. Augustine's *City of God* in its way marks the end of the ancient world in the west as clearly as do the great barbarian invasions.

# 2

# POETRY

The Latin epic had come to an end with the generation of Statius, Valerius Flaccus and Silius Italicus at the end of the first century A.D. Personal elegy, that peculiarly Roman creation, had ended with Ovid. There is no trace of significant dramatic writing, whether intended for the genuine stage or for 'concert performances', after Seneca. Juvenal was the last of the Roman satirists. Many of the principal genres of classical Latin poetry had thus virtually ceased to be practised before the great break in the middle of the third century. The great works of the past had become school-books, embedded in a mass of linguistic commentary and factual exegesis. The younger Pliny might dabble in lyric poetry in the Horatian manner, which his third wife set to music, but it is his letters that survive. The age of Hadrian, the Antonines and Septimius Serenus was one of prose. What little poetry was written is known to us only by fragments preserved by grammarians and metricians. Annianus and Septimius Serenus wrote on pastoral themes. Alfius Avitus composed a poem, apparently of some length, on Roman history. Marianus was author of a *Lupercalia*. These poets are called '*Poetae nouelli*' by the metrician Terentianus Maurus. Occasional poems by the historian Florus, by L. Aelius Verus and others survive, as well as Hadrian's famous address to his soul:

> Animula uagula blandula
> hospes comesque corporis,
> quae nunc abibis in loca
> pallidula, rigida, nudula,
> nec ut soles dabis iocos?

> *O blithe little soul, thou, flitting away,*
> *guest and comrade of this my clay,*
> *whither now goest thou, to what place*
> *bare and ghostly and without grace?*
> *nor, as thy wont was, joke and play.*
>
> (Tr. A. O'Brien-Moore in Magie (1921–32))

It is perhaps rash to base general judgements on so tiny a sample. But the work of all the writers mentioned appears to be marked by three striking characteristics. The first is the loosening of the link between form and content which has already been mentioned. Annianus' and Serenus' poems on the joys of country life follow neither the pattern of Virgil's *Eclogues* nor that of Tibullus' elegiac poems, but are written in a variety of metres. Avitus' poem on Roman history rejects the epic hexameter for the iambic dimeter, a metre found in the *Epodes* of Horace, and in choral passages in the tragedies of Seneca. The second trait common to these poets is metrical innovation, i.e. the creation of new metres by modification or combination of established patterns. Their third common feature is the abandonment of the traditional vocabulary of the various poetic genres and the use of vulgar, archaic, rustic, diminutive and other forms. Whether these poets formed a School or not is a matter of debate. But they all in various degrees appear to have rejected much of the classical tradition of Latin poetry and attempted to strike out in new directions. The few fragments surviving suggest an antiquarian taste, a baroque embellishment of the trivial, and a rather self-conscious avoidance of the grand manner and the solemn tone of voice. None of them appears to have been more than a gifted minor versifier.

In the period which is the subject of these chapters many of the trends marking the previous period continue to prevail. Minor subjects, a light, sometimes idyllic and sometimes frivolous tone, a taste for realism, are the order of the day at first. There are no long poems. The classical genres no longer impose themselves. But the elaborate metrical experiments of the later second century were abandoned, and most of what was written was in the well-tried hexameter or elegiac couplet. Most of the productions of the third century and the early fourth century cannot be securely dated; and sometimes the uncertainty extends even over more than a century. So there can be no question of reconstructing the history of poetry until we reach the second half of the fourth century. From the earlier part of the period we have a number of works, most of which can at best be dated somewhere between A.D. 250 and 350.

Marcus Aurelius Olympius Nemesianus of Carthage was the author of a didactic poem in hexameters on hunting, the *Cynegetica*, of which only the first 325 lines survive, and of four bucolic poems modelled on those of Calpurnius Siculus. Poems on fishing (*Halieutica*) and on sailing (*Nautica*) are also attributed to him, but do not survive. The *Cynegetica* can be dated to *c.* A.D. 284, and appears to draw on the Greek poem on the same theme by Oppian of Apamea in Syria, written in the first half of the third century. In spite of his avoidance of legendary material and his claim to originality, Nemesianus' inspiration is purely literary. The Eclogues embody traditional pastoral themes: lament for the death of an old shepherd-poet, rival shepherds singing the praises of their respective loves, Pan appearing to shepherds, a singing match between two shepherds. Both the *Cynegetica* and the *Eclogues* are full of Virgilian and Ovidian echoes. Some have seen in Nemesianus' poems some reference to the programme of political restoration attributed to the emperor Carus and his sons, but this is highly doubtful. Nemesianus is a competent and uninspired imitator of classical models, whose poetic persona is entirely traditional.

The mythological epyllion of Reposianus, *De concubitu Veneris et Martis*, in 182 hexameters, cannot be dated with certainty. It recounts the story of the amorous dalliance of Venus and Mars, first told in the Odyssey (8.266–360; developed by Ovid, *Ars Am.* 2.573–600, *Met.* 4.169–89) with an abundance of picturesque and on occasion slightly lubricious description. The tone is graceful and sentimental, but the poet is unable to convey any depth of feeling or to make his characters come to life. It has been suggested, but can be neither proved nor disproved, that the poem is an adaptation of a Greek original.

Six short elegiac poems by Pentadius are of equally uncertain date. The first, *De fortuna*, in 36 lines, proclaims with a series of illustrations from Greek mythology, each contained in a single couplet, the fickleness of fortune. The second, *De adventu veris*, in 22 lines, is an example of *versus echoici*; the first half of each hexameter is repeated in the second half of the following penta- meter, e.g.

> Laeta uireta tument, foliis sese induit arbor,
> uallibus apricis laeta uireta tument.

> *The joyous greensward swells, the trees put on their leaves,*
> *in the sunny valleys the joyous greensward swells.*

The remaining four poems are short epigrams. Pentadius' sole virtue is neatness.

A letter from Dido to Aeneas in 150 hexameters is a frigid piece of rhetoric stuffed with classical reminiscences. In the *Iudicium coci et pistoris iudice Vulcano*, in 99 hexameters, by an otherwise unknown Vespa the speeches of the two contendants are decked out with much rather obvious mythological learning. An anonymous poem in 89 hexameters sets out the speech of Achilles, hiding in the women's quarters, when he hears the trumpet of Diomedes. These and similar productions owe more to the schoolmaster than to the Muse. Their value, if they have any, is as indicators of the continuation of elements of the classical tradition of poetry in education. But everything in them is small in scale, mean in conception, and trite in expression.

The *Pervigilium Veneris* purports to be a processional song for a festival of Venus at Hybla in Sicily, in 93 trochaic tetrameters catalectic, with the recurring refrain

> Cras amet qui numquam amauit quique amauit cras amet.

> *Tomorrow he will love who never loved and he who loved will love tomorrow.*

It has been dated at various times from the second to the fifth century. Editors have argued that it is a work of the historian Florus, a contemporary of Hadrian, but without winning general assent. Unique in Latin literature, the poem recalls by its metre the acclamations of soldiers and populace at a triumph. There are also possible popular features in the syntax, though the vocabulary is largely classical. The simplicity of the style and the clarity of the descriptions confer an unusual freshness and charm on the poem. Typical are such passages as:

> Ecce iam subter genestas explicant tauri latus,
> quisque tutus quo tenetur coniugali foedere.
> subter umbras cum maritis ecce balantum greges.
> et canoras non tacere diua iussit alites.
> iam loquaces ore rauco stagna cygni perstrepunt.
> adsonat Terei puella subter umbram populi,
> ut putes motus amoris ore dici musico
> et neges queri sororem de marito barbaro.

> *Deeply bedded, look, the bulls in broom with massive flanks now lie.*
> *Every safety threading life must surely hail the marriage-tie.*
> *Bleating through the shadows, look, among the hes the bitches throng.*
> *Venus comes to tell the birds to be no niggards of their song.*
> *Raucous-crying swans go winging by and crash across the pool,*
> *and the nightingale is singing out where poplar-shades are cool.*
> *Surely it's a lover singing – one who sings a lover's joy –*
> *not a wandering sufferer who laments her sister and her boy.*
>
> (Tr. J. Lindsay, *Song of a Falling World* (London, 1948) 67–8)

Yet it is clearly a work of literary art and not an actual ritual song. There are many reminiscences of classical poetry. And there is no real religious ceremony at which it is likely to have been sung. It echoes the style and interests of the *Poetae nouelli* Annianus and Septimius Serenus (p. 10) though it may well have been written much later by an imitator or follower of their school.

To the same period of the late third or early fourth century belong the *Disticha Catonis*, a collection of about 130 (the number varies in different recensions) hexameter couplets each embodying a practical rule of conduct, e.g.

> Iratus de re incerta contendere noli,
> impedit ira animum, ne possis cernere uerum. (2)

> *Do not dispute in anger on a contentious matter;*
> *anger prevents your mind discerning the truth.*

The general tone is that of popular Stoicism, and there is no trace in the *Disticha* themselves of Christian attitudes, though a series of brief maxims in prose prefixed to the collection in many recensions shows Christian features. The author of the *Disticha* is unknown; the 'Cato' to whom they are attributed is Cato Uticensis rather than Cato the Censor. The collection is interesting as an echo of how the silent majority thought they ought to behave, and recalls the *Sententiae* of Publilius Syrus (*The Late Republic*, p. 119). What makes it worth mention in a history of literature is the enormous success which it enjoyed in the Middle Ages, when a number of different recensions, some interpolated, others abbreviated, circulated in hundreds of manuscripts, excerpts were embodied by many authors in their works, and translations and adaptations were made in the vernacular languages.

Publilius Optatianus Porfyrius, most probably an African, and to be identified with the *Praefectus urbi* in 329 and 333, addressed to the emperor Constantine in 325 or 326 a collection of twenty short panegyric poems, to which he later added seven others. Several poems in the Latin Anthology attributed to 'Porfyrius' are probably also by his hand. Porfyrius' poems, which appeal to the eye rather than to the ear, let alone to the mind, of the reader all involve complicated double or triple acrostics, lines which can be read backwards or forwards, words arranged according to the number of syllables they contain, and the like. His *tours de force* are his figurate poems, in the shape of a palm tree (9), a water organ (20), an altar (26) and a shepherd's flute (27). Such word games had been played by men of letters in their less serious moments since Hellenistic times. What confers on the poems of Porfyrius some importance in the history of Latin literature is that these trifles won the approval and patronage of Constantine, who deigned to address a letter of commendation to the ingenious versifier. Roman poets needed a patron but the level of taste at the imperial court in the early fourth century offered little hope of recognition to serious poetry.

Tiberianus, who may be identified with C. Annius Tiberianus, *comes Africae* in 325–7, *comes Hispaniarum* in 332–5, and Praetorian Prefect of Gaul in 336–7, is known as the author of four short poems – or fragments of longer poems. The first is a description in 20 trochaic tetrameters catalectic of an idyllic country scene, which recalls in metre and tone the *Pervigilium Veneris*. The others are an attack on the power of money in 28 hexameters, which draws its examples exclusively from Greek legend, a description in 12 hendecasyllables of the death of a bird, from which an edifying moral is drawn, and a hymn in 32 hexameters which is monotheistic but not specifically Christian. Tiberianus is an elegant and graceful poet, whose works were still read and quoted with approval by Servius in the fifth century. But it is difficult from the few fragments to form an idea of the scope and quality of his writing.

A poem in 85 elegiac couplets on the Phoenix is attributed to Lactantius in some manuscripts and by Gregory of Tours and may well be by his hand. It is in a rather inflated, rhetorical style, crammed with mythological references. In the Middle Ages it was taken to be an allegory of the Fall and Redemption of Man, but it is very doubtful if it was so intended by its author. There are no overt Christian references, though many passages are susceptible of a Christian interpretation, especially when separated from their context, such as the concluding line

aeternam uitam mortis adepta bono.

*Winning eternal life at the cost of death.*

The earliest major poem surviving from the fourth century is the *Evangeliorum libri* in four books by Gaius Vettius Aquilinus Juvencus, a Spanish priest of '*nobilissimum genus*', according to Jerome, written *c.* 330. It is also the earliest Latin poetry on a Christian theme, if we except the enigmatic poems of Commodian, which are variously dated by scholars. Unlike Commodian, who owes little to classical tradition and whose hexameters are half quantitative and half accentual, Juvencus remains firmly within the usage of classical epic. He writes for a readership which is mainly Christian, but which has studied Virgil, Horace, Ovid and Lucan and learnt to love them. His theme is the gospel story. His main source is Matthew, though he also draws on the other gospels, which he read both in the original Greek and in one of the pre-Hieronyman Latin versions. He concentrates on the main narrative and passes over the genealogy of Christ and the references to fulfilment of Old Testament prophecies. His language is the traditional epic *Kunstsprache*, enriched by occasional archaisms like *plebes, fuat, redimibit*, which are probably owed to a study of the grammarians of the Antonine age rather than to a direct familiarity with pre-classical Latin. Like the Greek historians of late antiquity he avoids the technical language of the church – *nuntius*, not *angelus* is his term for angel – and his neologisms are formed within the rules of epic language – words like *auricolor, glaucicomans, flammiuomus, altithronus*. His poem is full of echoes and flosculi of classical poetry, some of which are used for their deliberate effect. Thus in recounting the resurrection of Christ he uses the evocative phrase *in luminis oras*, which Lucretius borrowed from Ennius, Virgil from Lucretius and Valerius Flaccus from Virgil (Enn. *Ann.* 114, 131 V[2], Lucr. 1.22, Virg. *Geo.* 2.48, *Aen.* 7.660, Val. Flacc. 4.702). In his *praefatio* he takes up the traditional topic of the poet conferring immortality on those whose exploits he describes, and cites Homer and Virgil as examples. But he goes on to make the point that in his case it is the subject that will confer upon the poet such immortality as is possible in a transient world, and to call for inspiration not to Apollo and the Muses, but to the *sanctificus...spiritus*.[1] Juvencus is a conservative purist in matters of language and style, and the way in which he uses a highly traditional medium to treat a new theme is interesting. In particular his

---

[1] *sanctificus* appears for the first time in Juvencus, though *sanctificare* and *sanctificatio* had been used by Tertullian and clearly belonged to the technical language of the church (cf. Mohrmann (1961) 238). This use by Juvencus of a specifically Christian word in his invocation is not fortuitous.

personal involvement in the matters which he recounts leads to a change in the traditional persona of the narrative poet. It is no longer a mask concealing the man.

Juvencus sought to adapt the traditional form of didactic poetry to new purposes. Others continued to follow age-old models in form and content. Postumius Rufius Festus Avienius was a member of an ancient Italian family of Volsinii in Etruria, who numbered among his ancestors Musonius Rufus, the Stoic philosopher of the age of Nero and the Flavian emperors, teacher of Epictetus and the younger Pliny, and author of a manual of pagan theology in Greek. He was related to Valentinian's Praetorian Prefect Petronius Probus and held the proconsulships of Achaea and Africa probably a little after the middle of the fourth century, and his tombstone survives with a verse inscription celebrating his fame as a poet. Three didactic poems by Avienius survive: an adaptation in hexameters of the Greek astronomical poem of Aratus (*Phae-nomena*), a similar adaptation of the geographical poem of Dionysius Periegetes (*Descriptio orbis terrarum*) and the beginning of a poem on the sea-coast in iambic senarii, which describes the coast of Europe from Britain to Massilia (*Ora maritima*). The last is of particular interest since Avienius chose to adapt a Greek original of the fourth century B.C., and his poem therefore represents the earliest account we possess of western Europe. He was not a mere translator, but supplemented his sources with material from commentators, encyclopaedias and other sources. His style is smooth, classical and somewhat flat. His antiquarian interest is characteristic of the senatorial class of the fourth century, as is the maintenance of a poetic persona wholly detached from the age and circumstances in which the writer lived. The correct form of his name is given by an inscription. Until its publication he was generally known as Avienus. An epitome of Livy and a poem on the legends used by Virgil, both lost, and attributed by Servius to 'Avienus', are possibly the work of the fabulist known as 'Avianus', whose real name has recently been shown to have been Avienus and who wrote in the first half of the fifth century.

After this discouraging catalogue of poetasters and minor versifiers we at last reach in Ausonius a poet who can claim some stature, if only on account of the quantity and range of his writings. Decimus Magnus Ausonius was born in Bordeaux in 310. His father was a doctor, probably of Greek descent. His mother was descended on both sides from long-established aristocratic families of southwestern Gaul. Educated first at Toulouse by his uncle Arborius, who held a chair of rhetoric at Constantine's new capital city on the Bosphorus, and later at Bordeaux, the young Ausonius was appointed about 334 to an official teaching post in his native city, first as a grammarian and soon afterwards as a rhetorician. Thirty years later, when he had acquired a reputation as a teacher throughout Gaul, he was suddenly summoned to the imperial residence at

Trier to become tutor to Gratian, the six-year-old son of Valentinian. He remained attached to the court for some twenty years, accompanied Valentinian on his campaign against the Alemanni in 368–9, became a *comes* in 370, and *Quaestor sacri palatii* from 375 to 378. In the latter year he was appointed Praetorian Prefect of Gaul, while his son Hesperius was Praetorian Prefect of Italy, Illyricum and Africa. In fact, though Ausonius no doubt enjoyed considerable influence, the real power in Gaul was exercised by his son. In 379 he held the consulate along with Quintus Clodius Hermogenianus Olybrius, a member of a very distinguished Italian senatorial family who had had a long public career (and whose mother had some claim to literary fame as author of a Virgilian cento *De laudibus Christi*). After the murder of his pupil Gratian in 383 Ausonius returned to Bordeaux and lived there or on his estates in southern Gaul until his death in 393 or 394.

Ausonius provides an interesting example of the social mobility which literary distinction could bring in the fourth century. The son of a provincial doctor and of the daughter of a local notable, he not only became an influential member of the imperial court, but was accepted as an equal by the long-established senatorial aristocracy of Italy. His near contemporaries Libanius (*c.* 314–93) and Themistius (*c.* 317–88) provide similar evidence from the eastern half of the empire.

Ausonius wrote a great number of poems in many genres. Some are catalogue-poems, redolent of the school-room, such as the *Caesares*, the *Ordo urbium nobilium* 'List of notable cities', the *De nominibus septem dierum* 'The names of the days of the week' and the mnemonic poems on days of the week and months. Others are pieces of trivial virtuosity, like the macaronic poems in Greek and Latin ('Ελλαδικῆς μέτοχον Μούσης *Latiaeque Camenae* | ἄξιον Αὐσόνιος *sermone adludo bilingui*, etc.), the *Cento nuptialis*, the poems in which every line ends in a monosyllable, and so on. But there remains a considerable body of serious poetry on which Ausonius' fame rests. This includes: the *Parentalia*, in which he gives a brief account of the life and character of thirty deceased kinsmen or kinswomen, and the other poems connected with his family, in particular the funeral poem on his father and the poems addressed to his grandson Ausonius; the *Commemoratio professorum Burdigalensium* 'In memory of the professors of Bordeaux', in which he describes the person and career of twenty-six colleagues: the *Ephemeris*, describing the course of his daily round (incomplete); the short epyllion *Cupido cruciatus*; the seven poems on the German slave-girl Bissula, who had been given to him out of the booty of Valentinian's Alemannic war; the verse letters to his protégé and friend Paulinus of Nola; and the *Mosella*, a panegyric in 483 hexameters of the river, with many descriptive set pieces, composed in connexion with a journey which the poet made from Vingo (Bingen) to Augusta Trevirorum (Trier). Of his innumerable epigrams the great majority are displays of virtuosity or erudition, though a few show a sharp eye for the world around him. There also survive a number of prose works by him, mostly prefaces and letters, but including a long address of thanks to Gratian on the occasion of his consulship.

The chronology of Ausonius' writings presents many problems which are unlikely ever to be satisfactorily solved. The vast majority of the epigrams and technical *tours de force* from their nature contain no indication of date. Of the other poems some are dated by occasion or by reference to events, others by reference in a separate preface. But the date of publication of a poem is not necessarily the date of its writing. And Ausonius evidently reissued some of his poems in a revised edition. He seems to have published an edition of his opuscula about 383, and to have addressed a collection of poems to the emperor Theodosius in 390. But it is not clear what poems these collections included. The manuscript tradition does not point to a single, authoritative corpus of Ausonius' poetry. It is striking that we appear to have virtually nothing by Ausonius until he was in his later 50s. His extraordinary facility for extempore composition scarcely suggests a late vocation to poetry. Probably he did not deem some of his earlier works worthy of preservation (though one wonders when one reflects on what he did preserve). And much of his minor light verse was probably written, if not circulated, during his long years as a teacher in Bordeaux. Nevertheless it remains true that much of his poetry can be firmly dated in the seventh or eighth decade of his life, a period when the poetic vein in most men is wearing thin.

Ausonius was a Christian throughout most if not all of his life, and a few of his poems treat specifically Christian themes, e.g. the prayer in his *Ephemeris* 'Diary' and *Versus Paschales* 'Easter verses'. But he is not a Christian poet; his Christianity did not affect his poetic persona. When he composes a prayer in verse on the theme of his consulship it is addressed to Janus and to Sol. And the ideas and images which fill his poetry are entirely owed to traditional classical paganism. In his many poems on dead kinsmen and friends he makes no allusion to Christian hopes of an after-life. Only in the last poem (26) of the *Commemoratio professorum Burdigalensium* do we find a phrase capable of a Christian, as well as a pagan interpretation:

> sedem sepulcri seruet immotus cinis,
> memoria uiuat nominum,
> dum remeat illud iudicis dono dei
> commune cum dis[1] saeculum.  (11–14)

*May your ashes rest undisturbed in the tomb, but may the memory of your names live until there returns, through the gift of God who is judge, the age to be shared with the gods.*

[1] *cunctis* Baehrens; in which case the sense is 'the age which all will share alike'.

In the words of a perceptive French scholar, 'C'est un Chrétien, païen d'imagination et épicuréen de tempérament.'[1] Ausonius' changing relations with his young friend and protégé Paulinus of Nola will be discussed below (p. 35). Whatever lessons Ausonius the man may have learnt in the long and varied course of his life, Ausonius the poet shows no signs of intellectual, moral or aesthetic development. A prodigious memory, a facile talent for versification, a cheerful and kindly optimism, and an avoidance of all that was serious or profound or disquieting mark him throughout his literary life. In a century which saw the frontiers of the empire breached by barbarians, its ruling classes converted to a new religion which made urgent personal demands on its adherents, its ancient capital replicated in the middle of the Greek world, Ausonius appears to have retained at 80 the outlook and values of his youth. He is a man who, in the words of Dürrenmatt, passes through life without actually experiencing it. But within his rather narrow limits his excellence is striking. He can express everyday thoughts and emotions clearly, elegantly and with infinite variety. Completely at home in the classical tradition, he is never overwhelmed by it. Though his poetry is filled with conscious or unconscious reminiscences of Virgil, Horace, Ovid, Lucan, Statius, it is his own poetic voice that we hear. In a few poems, particularly those on Bissula and the *Mosella*, he displays a talent for sympathetic observation and strikingly vivid description which suggest that had he looked less at his books and more at the world about him he might have been a better poet. An example of his occasional capacity to see and describe something new is the scene of boys fishing in the river (*Mosella* 240–82) where the classical allusions and the traditionally structured simile are not mere external ornamentation, but serve to give sharper focus to the poet's vision.

> Iam uero, accessus faciles qua ripa ministrat,      240
> scrutatur toto populatrix turba profundo
> heu male defensos penetrali flumine pisces.
> hic medio procul amne trahens umentia lina
> nodosis decepta plagis examina uerrit;
> ast hic, tranquillo qua labitur agmine flumen,      245
> ducit corticeis fluitantia retia signis;
> ille autem scopulis deiectas pronus in undas
> inclinat lentae conuexa cacumina uirgae,
> inductos escis iaciens letalibus hamos.
> quos ignara doli postquam uaga turba natantum      250
> rictibus inuasit patulaeque per intima fauces
> sera occultati senserunt uulnera ferri,
> dum trepidant, subit indicium crispoque tremori
> uibrantis saetae mutans consentit harundo;

[1] Pichon (1906) 214.

nec mora, et excussam stridenti uerbere praedam     255
dexter in obliquum raptat puer; excipit ictum
spiritus, ut fractis quondam per inane flagellis
aura crepat motoque adsibilat aere uentus.
exultant udae super arida saxa rapinae
luciferique pauent letalia tela diei.     260
cuique sub amne suo mansit uigor, aere nostro
segnis anhelatis uitam consumit in auris.
iam piger inualido uibratur corpore plausus,
torpida supremos patitur iam cauda tremores
nec coeunt rictus, haustas sed hiatibus auras     265
reddit mortiferos expirans branchia flatus.
sic, ubi fabriles exercet spiritus ignes,
accipit alterno cohibetque foramine uentos
lanea fagineis alludens parma cauernis.
uidi egomet quosdam leti sub fine trementes     270
collegisse animas, mox in sublime citatos
cernua subiectum praeceps dare corpora in amnem,
desperatarum potientes rursus aquarum.
quos impos damni puer inconsultus ab alto
impetit et stolido captat prensare natatu.     275
sic Anthedonius Boeotia per freta Glaucus,
gramina gustatu postquam exitialia Circes
expertus carptas moribundis piscibus herbas
sumpsit, Carpathium subiit nouus accola pontum.
ille, hamis et rete potens, scrutator operti     280
Nereos, aequoream solitus conuerrere Tethyn,
inter captiuas fluitauit praedo cateruas.

*Here where the bank an easy access yields*
*A throng of spoilers through the river-depths*
*Are busy, probing everywhere (poor fish,*
*Alack, ill guarded by the inmost stream!);*
*One in mid water, trailing his moist lines*
*Far from the bank, sweeps off the finny droves*
*Caught in his knotted seine; another, where*
*The river floats along in tranquil course,*
*Spreads wide his drag-net buoyed on floats of cork.*
*A third, bent o'er the waters slumbering far*
*Beneath the boulders, dips the arching top*
*Of his lithe rod, casting upon the stream*
*Hooks sheathed with deadly baits. The wandering tribes,*
*Unwary, rush thereon with gaping jaws:*
*Too late their open mouths feel, deep within,*
*Stings of the hidden barb; they writhe; down drops*
*The float; the rod jerks to the quivering twitch*
*Of vibrant line. Enough! with one sharp stroke*

*The prey is hooked, and slantwise from the flood*
*The lad has flicked his prey. A hissing wind*
*Follows the blow, as when a lash is plied*
*And a wind whistles through the stricken air.*
*The dripping victims flounder on the rocks;*
*In terror of the sunlight's deadly rays*
*They quake; the fire that moved them while they lived*
*Down in their native element, expires*
*Beneath our sky; gasping, they yield up life.*
*Dull throbs go shuddering through their weakened frame;*
*The sluggish tail flaps in one final throe;*
*Mouths gape; the breath they drew returns again*
*In pantings linked with death. As when some breeze*
*Fans a forge-fire, the valve, that works within*
*The beechen bellows, first admits the wind*
*Then holds it, now by this vent, now by that.*
*Some fish have I beheld which, in their last*
*Death-struggle, have put forth their powers, to plunge*
*Head downward to the river; and so reached*
*The once despaired-of waters. Quick the lad,*
*Impatient of his loss, dives from above*
*And seeks to grasp them in his wild pursuit, –*
*A bootless quest! Ev'n so fared Glaucus once*
*(That old man of the sea); soon as his lips*
*Touched Circe's deadly herbs, he ate the grass*
*Sucked by the dying fish: then headlong leapt –*
*Strange denizen! – into Carpathia's main.*
*He that was wont, furnished with hooks and net,*
*To plunder Nereus in his watery realm,*
*Floats – the once pirate of those helpless tribes.*      (Tr. Blakeney (1933))

This passage displays Ausonius' sympathetic observation of everyday features of country life, and his ability to transform his observations by firm control and adaptation to a sophisticated literary tradition. Of the three fishermen two are described statically in neat couplets (243–6), the third is depicted at length in the process of catching and landing his fish (247–69). Ausonius is always skilful at varying the pace of his exposition. The poet goes on to comment in his own person on the difficulties attendant on rod-and-line fishing (270–5). There are two extended similes in the epic manner. The first (267–9) is entirely original, depending on the poet's own perception of the similarity between the movements of gills and mouth of a stranded fish and those of the valves of a blacksmith's double bellows. It is, incidentally, probably the first description in European literature of the double bellows, a technological development of late antiquity which made possible the casting of iron. The second (276–82) is an elaborate allusion to a Greek myth which had been recounted by Ovid, *Metamorphoses* 13.904–68. The whole passage is permeated by reminiscences of classical Latin poetry, varying from overt quotation to fleeting echo. Thus the picture of the various fishermen owes something to Virgil, *Georgics* 1.141–2 *atque alius latum funda iam uerberat amnem | alta petens, pelagoque alius trahit umida lina*; *letalia tela diei* (260) is a quaintly inverted echo of Lucretius' famous *lucida tela diei* (1.147); line 241 contains a purely verbal reminiscence of Statius, *Silvae* 3.2.86 *Siculi populatrix uirgo profundi* (of Scylla); in line 272 the rare word *cernuus* 'downward turned', 'head-over-heels', occurs in the same sedes in the verse as in Silius Italicus 10.255 *cernuus inflexo sonipes effuderat armo*. The whole passage is marked by an Ovidian neatness of expression, particularly in the numerous 'golden' lines (in which two nouns and their attendant adjectives are grouped in various arrangements round a verb), e.g. 241, 244, 246, 248, 249, 252, 254, 258, 263, 264, 266, 268, 278. Indeed the very frequency of these tightly-structured lines leads to a certain monotony. By way of more general critique of the *Mosella* and of some of his other poems, it may be observed that Ausonius is sympathetically responsive to man-made, 'tame' landscape, but blind to 'wild' landscape and to many aspects of nature. Thus birds and their song are not mentioned in the poem. There is nothing romantic in Ausonius' response to his surroundings.

Most of Ausonius' poems are in hexameters or elegiac couplets. But he also writes in a number of other metres, including some of those 'invented' by the writers of the Antonine age. Thus the brief epitaph on his aunt Veneria is in the resolved anapaests previously used by Septimius Serenus:

> ‿ ‿ ‿‿ ‿‿‿‿ ‿ ‿‿‿ ‿ ‿‿
> Et amita Veneria properiter obiit.
>
> *And aunt Veneria suddenly died.*

His prosody shows occasional departures from classical usage which mark the changing language of his age, such as *pālatia, parrīcida, tertiūs horum, omnĭum*. His vocabulary is firmly classical, with relatively few neologisms, all following classical patterns. His syntax shows only occasional late Latin features, such as *ad* + accusative for dative, *de* + ablative for genitive, comparatives formed with *magis*.

A collection of 72 poems, the *Epigrammata Bobiensia*, mostly in elegiac couplets, ranging from two to seventy lines, was discovered in 1950 in a manuscript in the Vatican Library. Some of these are attributed to Julius (or Junius) Naucellius, a friend and correspondent of Symmachus, probably born *c.* 305–10. A few others are by named authors and had been already published. The majority of the poems are without attribution. The first editor of the corpus believed that they were all the work of Naucellius, but this view has been challenged. They are brief occasional poems – descriptions of places and buildings, prayers, developments of popular ethical themes and the like. Dull and imitative, often clumsy in expression, they are a specimen of the trivial classicizing versification which passed for literature in some Italian senatorial circles in the later fourth century. Their dreary mediocrity brings out the relative brilliance of Ausonius, Naucellius' contemporary.

Ausonius, as we have seen, owed his career largely to his literary distinction. But his relation to Valentinian and Gratian was not that of client to patron, and few of his poems arose out of his dependence on his imperial protectors. With Claudian we move into the very different world of the professional poet who lives by his pen and most of whose poems were occasioned by events in the life of his patron. Claudius Claudianus, a native of Alexandria, was born about 370. We know nothing of his early career, but he had clearly studied rhetoric, and had probably found his vocation as a poet by the time he was twenty. About 394 he came to Rome to seek a patron and further his career. His earliest surviving work is a panegyric poem addressed to the consuls Anicius Probinus and Anicius Hermogenianus Olybrius, sons of the rich and influential senator Petronius Probus and his wife Anicia Faltonia Proba, and delivered at Rome in January 395. Claudian was no doubt adequately rewarded by his senatorial patrons and could have counted on other commissions from members of their extensive family in due course. But his panegyric – and perhaps other poems which we no longer possess – attracted the attention of a more powerful patron, the Vandal general Stilicho, husband of Serena, niece and adoptive daughter of the emperor Theodosius, and regent after his death on 18 January 395 for his ten-year-old son Honorius. The poet moved from Rome to the imperial capital at Milan, where he was appointed to the sinecure post of *tribunus et notarius*, thereby obtaining senatorial rank.

In early January 396 he recited his *Panegyric on the Third Consulate of Honorius*. From then until his death in 404 he was a kind of official poet laureate and propagandist for Stilicho, delivering panegyrics on official occasions, invectives upon Stilicho's enemies, and tendentious accounts of such public affairs as the war against Gildo in Africa. He may have travelled with Stilicho on his not very successful campaigns. But he did not return to Rome until early in 400, when he delivered before the Senate the third book of his panegyric on the consulate of Stilicho. On that occasion he received the singular honour of a bronze statue in the Forum of Trajan, set up by the emperor at the request of the Senate. The plinth still survives, in which Claudian is described in Latin as *praegloriosissimus poetarum* and is said in Greek to combine the mind of Virgil and the Muse of Homer (*CIL* VI 1710). Later in the same year he married the daughter of a wealthy African senator, thanks to the influence exerted by his patroness Serena. He apparently remained in Africa for some time on an extended honeymoon, but returned to Rome in time to recite a panegyric on the sixth consulate of Honorius in January 404. This is his last datable poem, and the probability is that he died in the course of 404. Otherwise he would scarcely have failed to celebrate Stilicho's second consulate in January 405.

This is virtually all we know of Claudian's life. Before going on to examine his poetry, there is one general consideration which springs to the mind. Claudian, who has often, and not unreasonably, been described as the last classical poet of Rome, was a Greek. Intellectual contact between the Greek east and the Latin west had been one of the casualties of the half-century of anarchy in the mid third century. The political unification of the empire under Constantine and his successors had done little to bridge the gap. It had been subject to interruption in the reign of Valens and Valentinian, and with the death of Theodosius in 395 the division of the empire became permanent. The Italian senatorial class and those who aped its life-style had more and more withdrawn from an imperial role – which involved some acquaintance with the Greek half of the empire – and knowledge of the Greek language and Greek thought had become rarer and more superficial in the west. By the time Claudian came to Rome the two halves of the empire had to some extent been going their separate ways in cultural matters for a century and a half. The occasional migrant from east to west like Claudian or his older contemporary the historian Ammianus Marcellinus brought to the Latin world a breath of the very different, and often more invigorating, air of the Greek east. Their problem was how to make an effective synthesis between the two cultural traditions, and not to remain outsiders in the west. We know how Ammianus acquired his knowledge of Latin and his understanding of Roman tradition; it was by long years of service in the army, often in western provinces and under western commanders, followed by private study in Rome. Claudian is more of an enigma. The evidence of papyri suggests an upsurge in the study of Latin language and literature in Egypt, as in other eastern provinces, in response to the foundation of a new imperial capital in the middle of the Greek world and the new career prospects which a knowledge of Latin offered. But it is a long way from word-for-word cribs to Sallust and Virgil to the superb command of literary Latin and the sympathy with traditional Roman ways of thought shown by Claudian. Perhaps he belonged to a bilingual family descended from a Roman official. Perhaps he had close associations with a Latin-speaking milieu in Alexandria. Be that as it may, he seems to have arrived in Rome already a more than ordinarily competent Latin poet.

But he brought more from Egypt in his baggage than a knowledge of Latin. If the Muses had long been silent in the west they had been unusually vocal in the Greek world, and in particular in Egypt, where the fourth and fifth centuries saw the flourishing of a school of poets. These poets travelled widely throughout the Greek cities of the empire, and took over many of the public functions which in earlier generations had belonged to rhetoricians. They were the spokesmen of their communities, reciting odes on official occasions, serving as propagandists for those in power, and both reflecting and creating public opinion. Two genres which they developed to a high pitch of technical perfection were the descriptive set-piece or ἔκφρασις and the panegyric, both of which had been treated in the third-century treatises of Menander as falling within the domain of rhetoric. Both of these genres normally made use of the language and style of post-Homeric epic. Claudian, who wrote poetry in Greek as well as in Latin – a Greek *Gigantomachia*, probably a youthful production, survives – brought with him to the west familiarity with the public role of the Greek poets of his time and a command of their technique of composition. Now the western world had been familiar with the prose panegyrical address since the days of Pliny the Younger, and a collection of twelve such prose panegyrics from the end of the third and the first two thirds of the fourth century survives (pp. 75–6). What Claudian did was to introduce to the Senate at Rome and the court at Milan the Greek practice of the poetic panegyric, first under the patronage of the Anicii, then under that of Stilicho. His success in fusing together the Greek genre and Roman habits of thought and allusion was such that the old prose panegyric – whose roots went back through classical rhetorical theory to the ancient Roman tradition of the *laudatio funebris* – died out completely. More than that, Claudian gave to Roman poetry a new vigour as well as new genres.

His surviving works, which run to close on 10,000 lines, fall into three main categories: panegyrics and other occasional poems, historical epics, and mythological epics. The first class includes the panegyric on Probinus and Olybrius of 395, those on the third, fourth and sixth consulates of Honorius, dated 396, 398 and 404 respectively, the panegyric on Stilicho of 400, the *laus Serenae* of 404, the epithalamium for the marriage of Honorius and Maria of 398, and that for the marriage of Palladius and Celerina, and the great invectives on the ministers of the eastern court Rufinus (397) and Eutropius (399). The second category comprises the *Bellum Gildonicum* of 398 and the *Bellum Geticum* of 402. To the third category belong the *De raptu Proserpinae* in three books, whose date is uncertain, and the unfinished Latin *Gigantomachia*, which was probably interrupted by the poet's death in 404. In addition there are a number of very short poems and epigrams on a variety of topics. The major poems are all written in hexameters, often preceded by a preface in elegiac couplets, a combination often found in Greek poetry of the period.

Though the distinction between the three categories of poems is clear enough, Claudian uses the same type of structure in all his longer poems. They are composed almost entirely of speeches and descriptive set-pieces, linked by the most slender line of narrative. The same structure is to be observed in much of the Greek poetry of late antiquity. Men had lost interest in sustained narrative on the grand scale, despite – or perhaps because of – the role played in education by Homer and Virgil. Personified abstractions play some role both in the epics and in the panegyrics and invectives. The figure of Roma in particular regularly appears. But there is no tendency towards sustained allegory. Indeed the episodic structure of Claudian's poems, in which successive speeches and ἐκφράσεις would each elicit a round of applause in public recitation, would make sustained allegory difficult. Claudian's strength – and what distinguishes his poetry from the rather loose and verbose compositions of contemporary Greek panegyrists – is his superb exploitation of all the tricks of rhetoric, his masterly use of the traditional language of Latin epic, with all its possibilities of allusion, and his unfailingly inventive imagination. And Claudian knows when to stop. His sentences and his paragraphs are tightly organized, and he scarcely ever yields, as Ausonius did, to the temptation to launch into a catalogue. In Claudian few words are wasted, yet every line contains a surprise.

What he has to say is largely drawn from Roman tradition. He was no original political or historical thinker, nor was he expected by his patrons to be one. Yet he knew how to select from the traditional amalgam just those commonplaces and those *exempla* which would put his patron's case in the best light, and how to vary his choice among traditional arguments to suit his audience, whether Senate at Rome or court in Milan. He was not just a technician of versification. Though much of his writing may seem bombastic to modern readers, it is bombast of a very high order – as a glance at the writings of his imitator Sidonius Apollinaris (q.v.) will show – and it clearly suited the taste of the times. He has many passages which are moving and impressive – reflecting feeling that was more than superficial – and a few which can stand comparison with the work of the giants of Latin literature. Examples are his eulogy of Rome in *Laudes Stilichonis* 3.130–60, the speeches of Rome and Africa at the opening of the *Bellum Gildonicum* (28–200), the description of the tapestry woven by Proserpine in *De raptu Proserpinae* (1.244–75). While he makes no attempt at suiting words or descriptions to character, he has at his fingertips the rhetorician's full range of 'stances' (*status*, στάσις). Thus the two invectives on eastern ministers adopt quite different tones. Rufinus is depicted as the embodiment of evil, malignant, threatening and powerful; Eutropius is treated as a buffoon and showered with ridicule and contempt. Strangely enough for a poet who devoted so much effort and skill to descriptions, Claudian has no visual sense. We do not know what Rufinus or Gildo looked like; and of Stilicho we know only that his hair was white (*Bellum Geticum* 459–60 *emicuit Stilichonis apex et cognita fulsit | canities*, probably the last passage of Claudian ever to be quoted in the House of Commons). Claudian's descriptive passages are based upon rhetoric and reminiscence, not upon observation. His poetry is shot through with echoes not only of Lucretius and Virgil and Ovid, but of Lucan and Statius and Silius Italicus. But he rarely quotes directly and he often fuses together reminiscences of two or more classical poets. Sometimes the classical echo was meant to add depth to his own expression. But it would be unwise to suppose that the Roman Senate or the imperial court could pick up and appreciate in the course of a recitation every fleeting allusion to earlier literature, as some scholars have tended to suggest. Rather he was himself so steeped in classical poetry that the quotations and allusions came unbidden to his pen. His deep familiarity with classical Latin poetry is reflected in his vocabulary, which has few neologisms, in his syntax, which is scarcely affected by the spoken language of his time, and in his prosody, which scarcely ever departs from classical rules, in spite of the tendency of living speech to neglect phonological distinctions of vowel length.

Claudian is described by Augustine as *a Christi nomine alienus* and by Orosius as *paganus peruicacissimus* (*Civ. Dei* 5.26, *Hist. adv. pag.* 7.35.21). Both men were his contemporaries, though neither can have known him personally. But it is by no means certain that they were right. He wrote an Easter hymn, *De Salvatore*, which is really rather a poem offering Easter wishes to Honorius. Otherwise his poetry has no trace of Christian expressions or allusions, and is filled with traditional references to the Olympians. But this is a matter of literature, not of life. It is striking that when Claudian first came to Rome he enjoyed the patronage of a senatorial family that had long been Christian, and that he then became court poet at the intensely Christian court of Honorius. He may well have been a nominal Christian. And if he was a pagan, his attachment would not be to the official cult of the Roman pantheon, which still had a powerful appeal to senatorial aristocrats like Symmachus, but to the Isis and Sarapis cults of his native Alexandria. In any case Christianity did not affect his poetic persona.

His 'official' poems appear to have been issued in a collected edition at the instigation of Stilicho between 404 and 408. The *Raptus Proserpinae* and the various minor poems survived separately.

The virtues and the shortcomings of Claudian's style may be exemplified by two passages, one of encomium, the other of invective.

> Proxime dis consul, tantae qui prospicis urbi,       130
> qua nihil in terris complectitur altius aether,

cuius nec spatium uisus nec corda decorem
nec laudem uox ulla capit; quae luce metalli
aemula uicinis fastigia conserit astris;
quae septem scopulis zonas imitatur Olympi;                 135
armorum legumque parens quae fundit in omnes
imperium primique dedit cunabula iuris.
haec est exiguis quae finibus orta tetendit
in geminos axes paruaque a sede profecta
dispersit cum sole manus. haec obuia fatis              140
innumeras uno gereret cum tempore pugnas,
Hispanas caperet, Siculas obsideret urbes
et Gallum terris prosterneret, aequore Poenum,
numquam succubuit damnis et territa nullo
uulnere post Cannas maior Trebiamque fremebat             145
et, cum iam premerent flammae murumque feriret
hostis, in extremos aciem mittebat Hiberos
nec stetit Oceano remisque ingressa profundum
uincendos alio quaesiuit in orbe Britannos.
haec est in gremium uictos quae sola recepit            150
humanumque genus communi nomine fouit
matris, non dominae ritu, ciuesque uocauit
quos domuit nexuque pio longinqua reuinxit.

*(Cons. Stilichonis* 3.130–53)*

*Consul, all but peer of the gods, protector of a city greater than any that upon earth the air encompasseth, whose amplitude no eye can measure, whose beauty no imagination can picture, whose praise no voice can sound, who raises a golden head amid the neighbouring stars and with her seven hills imitates the seven regions of heaven, mother of arms and of law, who extends her sway o'er all the earth and was the earliest cradle of justice, this is the city which, sprung from humble beginnings, has stretched to either pole, and from one small place extended its power so as to be co-terminous with the sun's light. Open to the blows of fate while at one and the same time she fought a thousand battles, conquered Spain, laid siege to the cities of Sicily, subdued Gaul by land and Carthage by sea, never did she yield to her losses nor show fear at any blow, but rose to greater heights of courage after the disasters of Cannae and Trebia, and, while the enemy's fire threatened her, and her foe smote upon her walls, sent an army against the furthest Iberians. Nor did Ocean bar her way; launching upon the deep, she sought in another world for Britons to be vanquished. 'Tis she alone who has received the conquered into her bosom and like a mother, not an empress, protected the human race with a common name, summoning those whom she has defeated to share her citizenship and drawing together distant races with bonds of affection.* (Tr. Platnauer (1922))

> Posteritas, admitte fidem: monumenta petuntur                    70
> dedecoris multisque gemunt incudibus aera
> formatura nefas. haec iudicis, illa togati,
> haec nitet armati species; numerosus ubique
> fulget eques: praefert eunuchi curia uultus.
> ac ueluti caueant ne quo consistere uirtus                        75
> possit pura loco, cunctas hoc ore laborant
> incestare uias. maneant inmota precamur
> certaque perpetui sint argumenta pudoris.
> subter adulantes tituli nimiaeque leguntur
> uel maribus laudes: claro quod nobilis ortu                       80
> (cum uiuant domini!), quod maxima proelia solus
> impleat (et patitur miles!), quod tertius urbis
> conditor (hoc Byzas Constantinusque uidebant!).
> inter quae tumidus leno producere cenas
> in lucem, foetere mero, dispergere plausum                        85
> empturas in uulgus opes, totosque theatris
> indulgere dies, alieni prodigus auri.          (*In Eutropium* 2.70–87)

*Ye who come after, acknowledge that it is true! Men must needs erect monuments to celebrate this infamy; on many an anvil groans the bronze that is to take upon it the form of this monster. Here gleams his statue as a judge, there as a consul, there as a warrior. On every side one sees that figure of his mounted on his horse; before the very doors of the senate-house behold a eunuch's countenance. As though to rob virtue of any place where she might sojourn undefiled, men labour to befoul every street with this vile image. May they rest for ever undisturbed, indisputable proofs of our eternal shame; such is my prayer. Beneath the statues one reads flattering titles and praises too great even for men. Do they tell of his noble race and lineage while his owners are still alive? What soldier brooks to read that single-handed he, Eutropius, won great battles? Are Byzas and Constantine to be told that this is the third founder of Rome? Meanwhile the arrogant pander prolongs his revels till the dawn, stinking of wine and scattering money amid the crowd to buy their applause. He spends whole days of amusement in the theatres, prodigal of another's money.*

(Tr. Platnauer (1922))

The first passage develops in majestic style some of the traditional topics of the *laudes Romae*, the poetic origins of which are to be sought in Horace's Roman odes and in Virgil's *Aeneid* (6.781–853), while for some of the matter Claudian is probably indebted to Aelius Aristides' Roman oration (*Or.* 26). A slightly later treatment of the same theme is to be found in Rutilius Namatianus, *De reditu suo* 47–164. The emphasis which both poets of late antiquity, the one writing before the capture of the city by Alaric, the other after that event, give to Rome's resilience after disaster underlines a preoccupation of the age. For Virgil there had been no such problem. Claudian carefully avoids verbal echoes of his Virgilian model. The varying rhythm of his hexameters, with their absence of end-stopping, the play with evocative words like *Cannae* and *Trebia* (at both of which Roman armies suffered a shattering defeat at the hands of Hannibal), the tight structure of the passage and the absence of ornamental words or padding, and the striking figure of Rome as a mother rather than a mistress (what Aelius Aristides calls the φιλανθρωπία of Rome (*Or.* 26.66)) combine to give to this tissue of commonplaces a seriousness of tone and a certain impressive grandeur.[1]

The second passage owes more to Juvenal than to Virgil. The apostrophes, the exaggerations, the unexpected turn which phrases take (*nimiae...uel maribus laudes* when the reader expects the much less effective point 'too much for a eunuch'), the dramatic rhetorical questions answered by the poet himself, are all part of the satirical manner. What is Claudian's own contribution is the tenseness of the structure, without a superfluous word, the careful arrangement, according to which the three rhetorical questions and answers are in order of increasing length, and the classical purity of the language, which recalls Virgil rather than Juvenal.

While Claudian brought new vigour and distinction to Latin poetry through his own brilliance and through the new attitudes and techniques which he imported from the Greek world, his older contemporary Prudentius pursued a very different course of innovation. The two poets are very likely to have known one another, and Prudentius had certainly read some of Claudian's works. Whether Claudian shows any acquaintance with Prudentius' poetry is still an open question.

Aurelius Prudentius Clemens, born in 348 in Hispania Tarraconensis – perhaps at Calahorra or Zaragoza – studied rhetoric and practised at the bar. Following a common career pattern in late antiquity he held two provincial governorships and a high office at the court of Honorius – perhaps that of *comes primi ordinis*. He spent some time in Rome. In 405 at the age of 57 he retired from public life to devote himself to writing devotional poetry. He may have become a member of an ascetic Christian community like the *servi Dei* to whom Augustine belonged. He left a corpus of poetry preceded by a preface and followed by an epilogue, and consisting of two cycles of poems in lyric metres: one of hymns for various times of the day, the other of hymns in praise of martyrs, all western and largely Spanish, two didactic poems in hexameters respectively on the doctrine of the Trinity and on the origin of evil, an allegorical poem in hexameters on the struggle between virtues and vices to possess the soul, a hexameter poem in two books replying to the *Relatio* of Symmachus, and a series of some fifty hexameter quatrains describing biblical scenes. The chronology of the poems is uncertain. His *Preface* suggests that Prudentius wrote them all after his retirement. But in fact some are likely to be of earlier date. In any case he must have written earlier poetry

[1] Cf. Cameron (1970) 352–61.

which he did not wish to survive, for his technical mastery points to long practice of the art.

Not since Horace had any Latin poet written such a substantial body of lyric verse, and Prudentius has been called the Christian Horace. He certainly knew Horace. But his use of lyric metres, often written κατὰ στίχον (that is, with every line repeating the same metrical pattern), owes more to the lyric passages of Seneca's tragedies and to the Antonine *Poetae novelli*. His long didactic poems (1,084 and 966 lines) have led some to see in him a Christian Lucretius. But though he has Lucretius' fervour, he lacks his powerful visual imagination and his pathos. His *Psychomachia* breaks new ground in being the first wholly allegorical poem in Latin. In it the virtues and vices fight it out in pairs like epic heroes. It was immensely popular in the Middle Ages and soon acquired a cycle of illustrations.

Prudentius takes over classical forms in language, metre and figures of speech without the body of classical allusion which traditionally accompanied them. His biblical characters and his martyrs do not appear in classical dress, his God is never *rector Olympi* or the like. He has few long descriptive passages. He dispenses with such conventions as the invocation, except in his *Preface*, where he gives it a Christian turn. And he introduces into Latin poetry an allegorizing pattern of thought derived ultimately from Christian interpretation of the Old Testament. At his best Prudentius writes with an economy and force equal to those of the classical models he so often imitates. But his prevailing vice is long-windedness and repetition. He is, accordingly, better in his lyric than in his hexameter poems.

His poetry, while not of first quality – how little was in late antiquity – is important as marking a new departure in Latin literature and a creative synthesis for his own purposes by a Christian poet from the amalgam of tradition, in which old forms are infused with new content, and in which the distinction between the poet as poet and as man is largely effaced. It is also indicative of the existence of a highly educated and refined reading public for poetry on Christian themes. In essence his audience probably coincided largely with that of Claudian. None of his poetry was intended for liturgical use, unlike, say, the hymns of Ambrose. (Though excerpts from the *Peristephanon* were later adopted by the Mozarabic liturgy.) And just as Prudentius' hymns are a literary reflection of those actually used in liturgy, so his poems on martyrs are a literary reflection of the artless accounts in the *Acta martyrum*, or of the short epigrams written by Pope Damasus to adorn the interior of churches. As a theologian he is insignificant: indeed he probably did not fully understand the heretical views which he sought to refute in his dogmatic poems. Prudentius' reply to Symmachus has sometimes been taken as evidence of a fresh struggle between Church and Senate over the famous altar of Victory in the

Senate House in Rome, after those of 381–4 and 392. It is better interpreted as a final refutation, based on the writings of Symmachus and Ambrose, of the whole ideology of the now dwindling group of pagan senators. Fervent Christian though he was, Prudentius treated those whom he attacked with respect and on occasion with magnanimity. Even the emperor Julian gets a word of praise from him. His reply to Symmachus – perhaps dead when the poem was written – displays a sense of measure and generosity not always present in religious polemic. It is entirely fitting that an edition of his poems should have been prepared in the sixth century for a descendant of Symmachus.[1]

Claudian and Prudentius each tried to do something new with a very old and by now rigid literary tradition. Others were content to work within that tradition. All were writing for the same audience, all adopted in some degree the same declamatory tone. Poetry in the late fourth and early fifth century was for public reading. At the same time others, who belonged to the same social class and shared the same culture, were making a conscious and deliberate break with the whole tradition in which they had been brought up. The two attitudes are embodied in two men whose lives must have spanned the same period, and who both belonged to that society of western magnates whose interests had gradually fused with those of the Italian senators, Rutilius Namatianus and Paulinus of Nola.

Rutilius Claudius Namatianus belonged to an aristocratic Gaulish family, possibly from Toulouse. The closing decades of the fourth century see the Gaulish landed families more and more drawn into the orbit of the Italian senatorial class.[2] Rutilius' father Lachanius had held a series of high offices, culminating in a prefecture. He himself became *magister officiorum c.* 412 and *praefectus urbi* in 414. In 417 he returned from Italy to his native Gaul where his estates had suffered in the invasion, and vanished from history.

His only recorded work is his poem in elegiac couplets describing his journey from Italy to Gaul. All that survives is the first book, of which the beginning is lost (644 lines) and the first 68 lines of the second book. In 1973 a further fragment of the second book, consisting of 39 half lines, was published from a piece of parchment which had been used to repair a Turin manuscript. The title of the poem was lost with the opening of Book 1. It has conventionally received the provisional title *De reditu suo*. The loosely structured poem describing a journey is a genre well established in Latin literature, from Lucilius' *Iter Siculum* (fr. 96–147 M) through Horace's *Iter Brundisinum* (*Sat.* 1.5), Ovid's journey to Tomis (*Trist.* 1.10), Statius' *Propempticon* (*Silv.* 3.2) to Ausonius' *Mosella*. The metrical form of Rutilius' poem suggests that Ovid was his particular model, and this is confirmed by the large number of Ovidian echoes. But Rutilius imports into the traditional genre much that

---

[1] Momigliano (1962) 216.     [2] Cf. Matthews (1975) 349–51.

is characteristic of the classicizing poetry of late antiquity, and in particular its declamatory tone. The digressions, which were traditional in the genre, are mainly in the form of speeches and descriptions, and the descriptions often turn into rhetorical soliloquies.

The poem in the form in which we possess it begins with an address to the reader on the greatness of Rome (1.1–46) and a long speech of farewell by the poet to the city, in which most of the traditional topics of the *laudes Romae* are rehearsed (1.47–164), and goes on to recount day by day the stages of the journey by sea from Portus Augusti (Porto) via Centumcellae (Civitavecchia), Portus Herculis (Porto Ercole), Faleria, Populonia, Vada Volaterrana, Portus Pisanus, to Luna, at which point the text breaks off. The description of each stage is accompanied by references to friends of the poet connected with the places passed or visited, and to their historical associations, as well as by personal reflections of the poet. The most noteworthy of these are his attack on the Jews (1.383–98), his invective against the monks of Capraria (1.439–52), his account of the life and virtues of his father (1.575–96), and his attack on Stilicho for 'betraying the secret of empire' and allowing Alaric and his Visigoths into Italy (240–60). These varied disgressions are designed to break the monotony of a necessarily repetitive narrative.

Rutilius has been generally held to have been a pagan, though a few scholars have argued that he must have been a nominal Christian. Be that as it may, his poetic persona stands firmly in the classical literary tradition and shows no sign of Christian ideas or expressions. Rutilius combines a sometimes moving reverence for ancient Roman tradition with an optimism concerning the future which takes in its stride Alaric's recent sack of Rome and the devastations of the Visigoths and the Bagaudae in his native Gaul.

Rutilius' predominating stylistic feature is parallelism and antithesis, often emphasized by patterns of alliteration or assonance. There is little enjambment between couplet and couplet, and few long periods. He has a gift – which recalls Juvenal – for expressing traditional and conventional ideas in striking phrases. Some of his verses are among the most memorable in Latin literature, e.g.

> Fecisti patriam diuersis gentibus unam;
>   profuit iniustis te dominante capi,
> dumque offers uictis proprii consortia iuris
>   urbem fecisti quod prius orbis erat.          (1.63–6)

*You made one fatherland for scattered nations; it profited the uncivilized to fall under your overlordship. In offering to those you conquer a share in your own rights you have made a city of what was formerly the world;*

or
> Vere tuo numquam mulceri desinit annus
>   deliciasque tuas uicta tuetur hiems.          (1.113–14)

*The year is unendingly caressed by your spring, and winter yields before your charms;*

or

> Illud te reparat quod cetera regna resoluit:
> ordo renascendi est crescere posse malis. (1.139–40)

*That which destroys other realms renews you: the secret of rebirth is to be able to grow by your own adversities;*

or

> Munera fortunae metuunt, dum damna uerentur:
> quisquam sponte miser, ne miser esse queat? (1.443–4)

*They are afraid of the gifts of fortune because they fear its penalties: does any man choose to be wretched in order not to be wretched?*

Rutilius' poem is studded with echoes and half-quotations – conscious or unconscious – not only of Virgil, Horace, Ovid and Juvenal, but also of his own contemporaries Ausonius and Claudian. His language and metre are classical, and show few concessions to the living tongue of his age.

Rutilius is a pleasing poet, elegant and often original in expression, capable of expressing depth of feeling on occasion, particularly when he dwells on the memory of Rome's greatness. His poetic persona moves in a limited world, but one within which he is entirely in control of his medium. The loss of at least half of his poem is regrettable. The new fragments are too brief and broken to add anything to our understanding of the poem, and are still the subject of controversy and discussion.

Meropius Pontius Paulinus, born *c.* 355 of a wealthy and noble family of Bordeaux, was a pupil and protégé of Ausonius, and began the languid career of intermittent public office typical of his class. After a mysterious personal crisis he and his wife took up the religious life, sold their vast estates, and ultimately settled at Nola in Campania, of which he became bishop *c.* 410 and where he died in 431.

Paulinus left a corpus of fifty-one letters and thirty poems, mainly in hexameters, but also in the lyric metres of Horace. Several of the poems are polymetric. Three, which date from before his conversion, are trivial personal or mnemonic poems in the manner of Ausonius (1–3). The rest are Christian in content. They comprise a panegyric on John the Baptist (6), paraphrases, with exegetical additions, of three of the psalms (7–9), verse epistles (10, 11, 22, 24), a propempticon for bishop Nicetas (17), a marriage poem or epithalamium (25), a consolatory poem on the death of a child (31), two protreptic poems (*Epist.* 8, poem 22), and thirteen poems written annually in celebration of the festival of St Felix between 395 and 407. A few fragments of other poems survive.

Paulinus distinguishes more clearly than any other poet of late antiquity between classical content and classical form, rejecting completely the former while adopting the latter. The whole universe of mythological allusion, which had supplied so much of the imagery of classical poetry, is excluded from his verse, its place being taken by biblical or hagiographic matter. Conventions like the invocation of the Muse are firmly rejected – *negant Camenis nec patent Apollini* | *dicata Christo pectora* 'Hearts dedicated to Christ reject the Muses and are closed to Apollo' (10.22–3) – and replaced by invocation of Christ (6.1ff., 21.672). His marriage poem banishes Juno, Cupid and Venus, condemns dancing, merriment and finery, holds up the example of Eve, Sarah, Rebecca and the Virgin Mary, and ends with a prayer that the marriage be not consummated or that if it is the children may adopt the religious life. Yet his verse follows classical models closely in metre and diction and is filled with echoes of classical poetry, which stand side by side with elements of specifically Christian language. Thus God is called both *tonans* and *creator*; *caro* is used of the incarnation; *Tartara* vies with *Gehenna*; technical terms like *euangelium*, *apostolus*, *mysterium*, *sacramentum*, *martyr* occur cheek by jowl with Virgilian *flosculi* like *nec inania murmura miscet* (10.121 ~ *Aen.* 4.201), *inlusas auro uestes* (25.43 ~ *Geo.* 2.464) or *odoratum nemus* (31.587, of Heaven ~ *Aen.* 6.685, of Elysium). Moreover Paulinus sets out clearly his poetic principle of taking over old forms with a new content in *Epist.* 16 and poem 22. His exchange of letters in prose and verse with his old teacher and friend Ausonius, who was shocked by his abandonment of his life-style and career, is a revealing and sometimes moving example of total lack of comprehension between two men apparently inhabiting the same intellectual world. (Auson. *Epist.* 23–31 Peiper.) Ausonius uses all the traditional arguments of the schools to re-establish contact while Paulinus replies in an anguished poem expressing the unbridgeable gap between them.

Though he displays the taste of his age for the declamation and the descriptive set-piece, Paulinus lacks the brilliance of Claudian and the neatness of Prudentius. His poems are inordinately long, and punctuated by digressions and personal reflections. He conveys the impression of one who does not know when to stop. The structural principle of his sentences is not antithesis and balance, but subordination. He composes in enormous clumsy sentences full of qualifications expressed in subordinate clauses of first, second and third degree, sentences which sometimes get out of control, which are never easy for the reader, and which must have been peculiarly difficult for those to whom they were recited aloud. His is no longer the confident, declamatory voice of the traditional poetic persona, but the slow, hesitant, private tone of one who thinks aloud, and who thinks about matters of supreme importance to himself. The poet and the man are no longer distinct. His attempt to preserve the classical forms while throwing overboard the whole of classical content had only limited success. His long-windedness, his didacticism, and his inability to vary his tone of voice put first-class poetry beyond his reach. His literary culture and his spiritual enthusiasm never fully fused together.

His letters are mainly on religious matters. Those to Ausonius, and the long 16th letter to Jovius on the relation between Christianity and classical culture are of more general interest.

Though in the eyes of Augustine Paulinus was an authority on Plato, he had, like most of his generation, only a superficial acquaintance with Greek culture, acquired during his schooldays.

One of the participants in Macrobius' *Saturnalia*, whose sole contribution to the dialogue is a series of amusing anecdotes, is a young man called Avienus. He is probably to be identified with the Avianus or Avienus (the orthography in the manuscripts varies) who about 430 dedicated a collection of forty-two fables in elegiac verse to a certain Theodosius, the name by which Macrobius was known to his contemporaries. Most of the fables were taken over from Babrius via the lost Latin prose translation by Julius Titianus, a third-century rhetorician, and a few come from another now lost Latin Aesopic source; there is no evidence that Avianus knew Greek. Elegiac verse, organized in discrete couplets, is ill suited to the narrative structure of fables. And Avianus has little poetic talent. His style is pompous and often obscure, and loaded with reminiscences of Virgil and Ovid. His Latinity, in spite of his efforts at classicisms, displays many features of the spoken tongue of his time, e.g. indirect statement with *quod*+subjunctive, *necdum* in the sense 'no longer', *diurnus* = *quotidianus*, and much inept anacoluthon. In spite of his short-comings, Avianus enjoyed immense success as a moralist in the Middle Ages. He is probably the author of a lost epitome of Livy and a poem on legends in Virgil attributed by Servius (*Aen.* 10.272, 388) to 'Avienus'. His work is an example of the trivial versification in imitation of classical models which was valued as an accomplishment in senatorial circles in the fifth century.

Yet even in the turbulent fifth century literary talent could open the way to high office. Flavius Merobaudes, a Spanish rhetorician, made his way to the court of Valentinian III at Ravenna and tried to do for Valentinian and Aetius what Claudian had done for Honorius and Stilicho. He was rewarded with the dignity of *comes sacri consistorii* and a statue set up in 435 in the forum of Trajan at Rome, the base of which, with its laudatory inscription, still survives (*ILS* 1 2950). In an age of war and invasion he had to wield the sword no less than the pen – *inter arma litteris militabat et in Alpibus acuebat eloquium* 'In the midst of arms he served letters and sharpened his eloquence in the Alps' – and reached the rank of *magister utriusque militiae*, commanding an army in Spain in operations against the Bagaudae. All that survives of his work is a series of purple passages excerpted by a later connoisseur. These include two ἐκφράσεις (descriptive set-pieces) of mosaics in an imperial palace or villa, in which Valentinian and his family were depicted, a short poem in hendecasyllables on the birthday of Aetius' infant son Gaudentius, part of a prose panegyric on Aetius' second consulate in 437 and a verse panegyric on his third in 446 (of which about 200 hexameters are readable), and a short poem on Christ. Merobaudes models himself on Claudian and Statius. He handles classical Latin and classical allusion with neatness and even elegance, but he lacks the force of Claudian and his inventive verbal imagination. The torch of classical tradition was clearly burning rather low in fifth-century Ravenna. The main interest of his poems today is as historical sources for a period in which the historian is ill served.

Yet in neighbouring Gaul, despite the establishment of Visigothic and Burgundian kingdoms in a large part of the province, a society of rich senatorial landowners not only maintained Roman culture in the fifth century but even re-established some intellectual contact with the Greek east. Knowledge of Greek was not uncommon, and could be more than merely superficial or school-based. Men read Plotinus and Porphyry and the Greek Fathers. They were interested in Greek astronomical and astrological learning. They translated Philostratus' *Life of Apollonius of Tyana*, with its clear message that the moral virtues are independent of the Christian faith. It is against the background of this short-lived Greek renaissance that we must view the life and work of Sidonius Apollinaris.

Gaius Sollius Apollinaris Sidonius was born in Lyons about 431 of a very wealthy senatorial family of Auvergne. Both his father and his grandfather had been Praetorian Prefects of Gaul. Educated in grammar and rhetoric at Lyons and probably at Arles, where public schools seem to have continued to exist, he was married in 451 to the daughter of another aristocrat from Auvergne, Flavius Eparchius Avitus, who had close connexions with the Gothic court at Toulouse. In 455, after the Vandal sack of Rome and the lynching of the ineffectual emperor Petronius Maximus, Avitus was proclaimed western Roman emperor at Arles. Sidonius accompanied his father-in-law to Rome and delivered a verse panegyric upon him, for which he was rewarded by the now customary statue in the forum of Trajan. The Italian aristocracy, the eastern court, and the Frankish general Ricimer made common cause against Avitus, and in October 456 he was obliged to abdicate and accept a bishopric. Sidonius was in danger for a time but soon made his peace with the new emperor Majorian, on whom he pronounced a panegyric in 458 when the emperor came to Lyons. Appointed *comes*, he accompanied Majorian on his campaigns until his assassination in 461. Sidonius then returned to Gaul and spent some years in private study, the management of his estates, and the *dolce vita* of the late Roman aristocrat. When in 467 the eastern emperor Leo appointed Anthemius, a Greek and a Neoplatonist, to the imperial throne of the west, Sidonius was sent on a mission to the new ruler by the Gaulish aristocracy. In 468 he delivered a panegyric upon Anthemius and was appointed by him *Praefectus urbi*. The hostile demonstrations of the hungry inhabitants of the Eternal City were not to the taste of a Gaulish magnate, and as soon as he could Sidonius escaped to the peace of his estates in Auvergne, dignified by the rank of *patricius*. Things were not going well in Gaul. The Visigothic king Theodoric had been succeeded by his son Euric, who was eager to extend his territory at the expense of the Romans. The great landowners governed their own territories in virtual independence of the central government. Peasant revolts were brewing. Sidonius now seems to have spent more and more of his time in the company of bishops and other clerics, who offered the hope of a kind of stability and continuity.

In 471 he was elected bishop of the Arverni, with his seat at Clermont-Ferrand, perhaps after a few months in lower ecclesiastical orders. Several of his kinsmen and friends entered the church at about the same time. In 472 King Euric attacked Auvergne. Although many of the Gaulish aristocracy sided with the Visigoths in the hope of retaining their estates Sidonius headed the resistance to the invaders. It was in vain. In 475 Auvergne was ceded to the Goths, and Sidonius became the subject of a barbarian king. Imprisoned for a time, he purchased his freedom at the price of a short panegyric on Euric. In 476 he returned to Clermont, where he devoted himself to administering and leading his diocese until his death in 486. He was later canonized.

His surviving works consist of twenty-four poems, in an edition prepared by the author in 469, and *c.* 150 letters in nine books. The poems are divided into *Panegyrici* (poems 1–8) and *Nugae* (poems 9–24). The *Panegyrici* begin with the panegyric on Anthemius in 548 hexameters (1) preceded by a preface in elegiac metre. There follow the panegyric on Majorian in 603 hexameters (5) preceded by two short prefatory poems, that on Avitus in 602 hexameters (7) with its preface, and a short elegiac poem addressed to Priscus Valerius, a kinsman of Avitus and former Praetorian Prefect of Gaul. The *Nugae*, in hexameters, elegiac couplets or hendecasyllables, comprise addresses to friends, two epithalamia, descriptions of buildings and works of art and the like. They vary in length from 512 lines to 4. A number of further short poems – including that in honour of King Euric – are contained in the letters. The letters are not real items of correspondence, but rhetorical set-pieces. In his preface he says that he imitates Pliny and Symmachus rather than Cicero, and describes his epistles as *litterae paulo politiores*. They are thus full of the commonplaces of ancient epistolography. The earliest of the letters, the description of King Theodoric (*Epist.* 1.2) dates from 455–60; the remaining letters of Book 1 are connected with Sidonius' mission to Rome in 467. The book was probably published in the following year. Thereafter there are few sure indications of date, and it is clear that the letters are not arranged in chronological order. Books 2–7 were probably published in 477, Book 8 in 479, Book 9 in 482. Apart from these indications each letter has to be dated by internal evidence.

Sidonius' style, both in verse and in prose, is inflated and precious, full of word-plays, complex figures of speech, mythological and historical allusions, to which is added biblical imagery in the letters written after his assumption of the bishopric. He is a man of considerable learning, though he not infrequently gets things wrong. For him, as for the other aristocrats who compose his world, literary culture is the outward and living sign of his Romanity, which he sees threatened by a tidal wave of barbarism. Yet like other members of his class he is ready to come to terms with the new rulers in the hope of retaining something of his economic and social position. He praises one of his friends for his perfect knowledge of Gothic. His entry into the church was the only way out of his dilemma. As a bishop he was the defender of a culture in which the Goths too, Arians though they were, could share. And he was able to continue the role of paternalistic leadership which his family had exercised in his province for generations. His prestige and influence in Romania and Gothia alike were immense. Today he is of interest primarily as a priceless historical source. Few would read Sidonius for his literary merit. Yet behind his often absurd preciosity lies a real talent for description and narrative. His descriptions of the Visigoths (*Epist.* 1.2, poem 23, *Epist.* 5.12, 6.6, 33, 8.9), the Burgundians (poem 12), the Franks (poem 5.237ff., *Epist.* 4.20), the Saxons (*Epist.* 86) and the Huns (poem 2.243ff.) show sharp observation which goes beyond the commonplaces of the genre. His account of the 'satire' of Arles (*Epist.*1.11), of the trial of Arvandus (*Epist.*1.7), of the adventures of the reader Amantius (*Epist.*7.2) show him a superb raconteur.

For all his limitations – and he scarcely seems to have noticed Romans who did not belong to his own class – Sidonius is an attractive character and on occasion an attractive writer. We know that he lived through the decline and fall of the western Roman empire. This was knowledge denied to him. But he tried to keep his head in difficult circumstances, and in a large measure succeeded.

Ausonius' grandson Paulinus of Pella had to face the same problems as Sidonius, but with inferior resources both personal and material. Born at Pella in Macedonia during the praetorian prefecture of his father Hesperius, he was soon brought to Bordeaux where his education, in both Greek and Latin, was supervised by Ausonius. For a number of years he lived the idle life of a selfish aristocrat, a Sidonius without Sidonius' cultural interests. In 396 he married, without much enthusiasm, a rich heiress. This life of ease was interrupted by the Gothic invasion of 406, when Bordeaux was sacked and Paulinus lost much property. He left Bordeaux for the more defensible Bazas, which in its turn was besieged by the Goths. Paulinus raised the siege by coming to terms with the Goths' allies the Alans, a compromise which many Romans regarded as treasonable. His position was not improved by his accepting office under the puppet emperor Attalus in 410. For a time he thought of returning to the tranquillity of the east, or becoming a monk, but both projects were resisted by his wife. For many years he lived in relative poverty on a farm near Marseilles, and later returned to Bordeaux to a similar small estate. More and more alone as his family died one by one and prevented by age from running his farm, he was saved from destitution by a Goth who gave him a good price for it, paid in cash.

In his eighty-fourth year he wrote a curious autobiographical poem, the *Eucharisticon Deo sub ephemeridis meae textu* 'Thanksgiving to God in the form of my diary'. The memories of his long life come tumbling out in his clumsy tortuous Latin. Paulinus was no scholar or man of letters, but was driven by an urge to examine his own life. His message is to thank God that things might have been worse. Virgilian tags from his schooldays spring to his pen, but there is very little else of classical tradition in matter or manner, and his striving for self-revelation is the antithesis of the classical poetic persona. He has no animus against the Germans. Paulinus' poem provides a fascinating picture from an upper-class point of view of the disintegration of a traditional society.

# 3

## BIOGRAPHY

The form of imperial biography established in the second century by Suetonius continued to be followed during late antiquity, and was later adopted as a model by Einhard for his *Life of Charlemagne*. Of other classical forms of biography, such as the life of the philosopher, there is no trace in the Latin west, though the Greek east provided excellent examples in the *Life of Plotinus* by Porphyry (*c*. 234–*c*. 305) and the *Lives of the Sophists* by Eunapius of Sardis (*c*. 345–*c*. 414). The *vie romancée*, whether its aim was to instruct or to amuse, is represented by a single translation from a Greek original, the *Res Gestae Alexandri Magni* of Julius Valerius.

The expansion of Christianity in the fourth century transformed or revivified many classical literary genres to fulfil its own purposes. Thus Eusebius originated a new type of history, in which the methods and skills of the antiquarian were united with those of the rhetorician, which had dominated historiography since Hellenistic times. So too in biography Athanasius struck out in a new direction with his *Life of Anthony*, which provided the model for lives of holy men and bishops for centuries. Latin writers soon took up the new genre, as for example in Jerome's *Life of Paul*, an entirely fictitious biography of an alleged predecessor of Anthony (*MPG* 23.17–28). The *Life of Cyprian* which survives under the name of Pontius is, at any rate in its present form, not the third-century text which it purports to be.

Marius Maximus, who is probably to be identified with Lucius Marius Maximus Perpetuus Aurelianus, consul for the second time in 223, wrote twelve biographies of the emperors from Nerva to Elagabalus (†222). His work, along with that of Juvenal, was avidly read by those late fourth-century Roman aristocrats whose libraries were usually kept closed like tombs (Amm. Marcell. 28.4.14). The biographies have not survived, and it is sometimes hard to know how much credit to attach to statements about them in the *Historia Augusta*. They seem to have followed in style and treatment, as in number, the *Lives* of Suetonius, i.e. the activities of an emperor after he attained power, which inevitably form the bulk of an imperial biography, were treated not chronologically, but by categories arranged in an elaborate system of dichotomies. What we cannot be sure of is whether Marius Maximus really wrote at much greater length than Suetonius – he is called *homo omnium uerbosissimus* by *S.H.A. Firm.* 1.2 – or whether he included more documentary material. He seems to have had, in an even higher degree than Suetonius, a taste for trivial and occasionally scabrous details. But he was clearly a thoughtful writer who used his own judgement, and, within the limits imposed by the genre, a reliable source. There is no reason to believe, however, that he had the access to material in the imperial archives which confers particular historical value on Suetonius' *Lives*. His popularity seems to have been shortlived. He is not quoted by later writers except in the *Historia Augusta*.

The *Historia Augusta* is a collection of lives of emperors from Hadrian to Numerian, dealing not only with reigning emperors, but with co-emperors and pretenders as well. It is likely that Lives of Nerva and Trajan have been lost from the beginning. The title was given by Isaac Casaubon, who published the *editio princeps* in 1603. The manuscripts have variations on the theme 'Vitae diuersorum principum et tyrannorum a diuo Hadriano usque ad Numerianum a diuersis scriptae' 'Lives of the various Princes and Usurpers from Hadrian to Numerian written by divers hands'. There are thirty biographies in all, some dealing with groups of emperors or pretenders. They are addressed to Diocletian, Constantine and various personages of their period, and purport to have been written at various dates from before 305 till after 324. They are attributed to six authors, of whom nothing else is known: Aelius Spartianus (7 lives), Julius Capitolinus (9), Vulcatius Gallicanus (1), Aelius Lampridius (4), Trebellius Pollio (4) and Flavius Vopiscus (5). The lives range in length from 49 printed pages (Severus Alexander) to 6 (Antoninus Geta), though in the composite biography entitled *Tyranni Triginta*, 'The Thirty Tyrants', 'Trebellius Pollio' polishes off thirty-two alleged pretenders in exactly as many pages. The arrangement of the lives is Suetonian, in that each author recounts his subject's life chronologically until he becomes emperor, and thereafter by categories – public life and private life, war and peace, at home and abroad, and so on – until with the approach of his death the chronological method takes over again. The lives contain more documents, letters, speeches, laws and the like, than those of Suetonius, and at least as much curious anecdotal information on the personal lives of their subjects – Firmus ate an ostrich a day (*Firm.* 4), Maximus consumed a 'Capitolina amfora' of wine and 40 pounds – or as some say 60 – of meat per day (*Maximini duo* 4), Tacitus on the other hand entertained a convivium with a single chicken eked out with eggs, and rarely took a bath (*Tac.* 11), Elagabalus had tame lions and leopards which were trained to take their places at the dinner-table, to the discomfiture of the guests (*Heliog.* 21). Many otherwise unknown authorities are quoted, some for their writings, others for information supplied orally.

Since its first publication the *Historia Augusta* has been recognized to be a particularly unreliable source. The majority of the numerous documents which it contains were soon shown to be false. No differences in language and style could be detected between the six authors. The distribution of the various Lives between them was found capricious. And there were inconsistencies – Spartianus in his Life of Niger (8.3) claims to be about to write the Life of Clodius Albinus, but that Life is actually attributed to Julius Capitolinus. Readers saw more and more apparent allusions to persons and events of the later fourth century in these Lives allegedly composed at the beginning of the century. And verbal echoes of the *Caesares* of Aurelius Victor, published in 360, and of the *Breviarium* of Eutropius, published in 370, suggest dependence on these works, since neither Aurelius Victor nor Eutropius was in the habit of copying out his sources verbatim. But no systematic explanation of the cause or nature of the unreliability was offered by scholarship until the late nineteenth century, when it was argued that the whole work was a forgery, written by a single hand towards the end of the fourth century, and reflecting the views and events of that period. Attempts to defend the authenticity of the *Historia Augusta* by postulating a later edition or a series of editors have in general foundered, as has the suggestion that it was a work of propaganda on behalf of the emperor Julian. Today most scholars accept that the work is a piece of deliberate mystification, written much later than its purported date, though the fundamentalist position still has distinguished support. Those who believe the *Historia Augusta* to be a forgery are not in agreement on its purpose. Some argue that the work is a piece of propaganda, probably connected with the pagan senatorial reaction at the end of the fourth century. Others point out that the political views expressed in the lives are trivial and that it is better seen as a hoax, the product of the eccentric imagination of some maverick *grammaticus*, to be compared with the roughly contemporary correspondence of Seneca and St Paul (cf. Appendix) or the later historical fantasies of Geoffrey of Monmouth. No solution to the problems presented by the *Historia Augusta* is ever likely to satisfy all critics. Too much depends on subjective valuation. And it is never easy to determine whether an error or absurdity is better explained as the result of misunderstanding or imposture. Knaves and fools cannot always be distinguished a millennium and a half later.[1]

Be that as it may, the value of the collection for the historian depends largely on the sources used. As has been observed, a great many authorities are quoted whose existence can be neither proved nor disproved, since they are

---

[1] Cf. Appendix, for a brief history of the controversy on the nature and date of the *Historia Augusta*.

otherwise unknown. Marius Maximus is often quoted in the earlier lives, the longer of which on the whole contain more verifiable material and fewer absurdities and improbabilities than the later lives, or the shorter lives of Caesars, short-lived emperors and usurpers. Marius' imperial biographies were certainly an important source, perhaps the principal source, for the main lives from Hadrian to Elagabalus. The shorter lives in this section are largely composed out of bits and pieces from the longer lives, supplemented by invention – in Mommsen's words 'nicht etwa eine getrübte Quelle, sonder eine Kloake' 'not so much a troubled spring, rather a sewer'. There may well have been a second biographical source available for the early lives; the hypothesis that they also drew on a lost annalistic historian of the Severan age has by now been generally abandoned. For the later lives the postulate of a lost narrative history, dating perhaps from the time of Constantine, still stands though shakily. The same source may also have been used by Eutropius and Aurelius Victor. But its authorship, structure and tendency remain unclear. Much of the rest of the material in the later lives, including the many fictitious pretenders, must be put down to imagination and inventiveness, backed up by wide reading and a retentive memory. Occasionally one sees, or fancies one sees, how the author's mind worked: *Memmia, Sulpicii consularis uiri filia, Catuli neptis*, the unconfirmed and probably fictitious second wife of Alexander Severus (*Alex.* 20.3), is almost certainly derived from the description of Sulpicius Galba's wife in Suetonius, *Mummiam Achaicam, neptem Catuli* (*Galba* 3.4).

It is hard to attribute an ideology to the *Historia Augusta*. Its good emperors are those who govern along with the Senate. But this is traditional political wisdom rather than a practical programme for the fourth century. The work in its present state has no general preface. There are secondary prefaces to the Lives of Macrinus (in which the probably fictitious biographer Junius Cordus, who had already appeared in the Life of Clodius Albinus under the guise of Aelius Cordus, is formally introduced), of the two Maximini, of the three Gordians, of the Thirty Tyrants, of Claudius, of Aurelian (in which the author recounts how Iunius Tiberianus promised to obtain for him from the Bibliotheca Ulpia the *libri lintei* in which Aurelian had kept his diary), Tacitus, Probus (in which he sets out in impressive detail a list of fictitious sources), of Firmus, Saturninus, Proculus and Bonosus, and of Carus and Carinus (in which he gives a bird's-eye view of Roman history from the foundation of the city). But only in the preface to the Life of Claudius does the author expressly discuss the qualities of the ideal emperor. They are hardly the result of profound political thought or intense partisan feeling. He must combine the *uirtus* of Trajan, the *pietas* of Antoninus, the *moderatio* of Augustus, and so on. While the *Historia Augusta* is written from a pagan point of view, it is not concerned with anti-Christian polemic. Indeed it is probably too frivolous a work to have any serious political or religious message.

The style is in general simple and unrhetorical, recalling that of Suetonius. It lacks the strident, declamatory tone of much fourth-century Latin prose, to which the author(s) rise(s) only in some of the prefaces.

Probably written by a practical joker for entertainment rather than information and aiming to titillate and satisfy the interest of readers preoccupied with details of the private life of the great and powerful, the *Historia Augusta* is also, unfortunately, the principal Latin source for a century of Roman history. The historian must make use of it, but only with extreme circumspection and caution. Other readers are drawn to this extraordinary work by curiosity rather than by a taste for literary excellence. Those whose taste inclines towards speculation on the psychology of the impostor will find in the *Historia Augusta* much food for thought.

To the category of *vie romancée* belongs the Alexander-Romance of pseudo-Callisthenes, a strange amalgam of history, fantasy and dead political pamphleteering. First put together in Greek, perhaps in the third century A.D., the original text has been translated, modified and supplemented many times through the centuries, and versions in the vernacular are known from places as far apart as Iceland and Java. The earliest Latin version was written in the closing decades of the third or the opening decades of the fourth century by one Julius Valerius (Alexander Polemius). He has been tentatively identified with Flavius Polemius, one of the consuls of 338; but it would be safer to admit that we really know nothing of his person. His text is a translation of a Greek version akin to but not identical with Version A.[1] He writes with some pretension to elegance of style. But his Latin is full of strange words like *anguina* ( = *anguis*), *equitium* ( = *equites*), *extuberasco, furatrina* (elsewhere only in Apuleius), *inconspectus, intranatabilis, lubentia, supplicialis,* and of unclassical constructions like the genitive of comparison (*tui sollertiorem*), *habere* + infin., *impendere* + accus., *laudare aliquem alicuius rei, prae* + accus. This suggests the work of a provincial rhetorician, perhaps more at home in Greek than in Latin, rather than of a scholar or a member of a learned senatorial circle.

Julius Valerius' text was used by the unknown author of an *Itinerarium Alexandri* dedicated to Constantine. This is a very rough summary of Alexander's campaigns, based partly on Arrian and partly on Julius Valerius, and without any pretension to literary merit.

The Metz Alexander Epitome represents the *disiecta membra* of another Latin version of the Alexander-story. In its present form it tells the story of Alexander's life from just after the death of Darius to the Indian campaign, and then goes on to recount the plot to poison the king, his death, and the

[1] Ed. Kroll (1926).

terms of his testament. The first portion is based directly or indirectly on Diodorus and Quintus Curtius, i.e. it represents historical rather than legendary tradition. The second portion corresponds closely to that of the early versions of pseudo-Callisthenes. The work cannot be dated with certainty, but belongs to late antiquity rather than to the Middle Ages. All these works testify to the attraction which the personality and exploits of Alexander – real or imagined – had for the men of late antiquity. It is no wonder that John Chrysostom (*Ad illum. catech.* 2.5 (2.243E)) upbraided the Christians of Antioch for using coins of Alexander as amulets.

It should be noted that none of these early Latin versions provided the starting-point for the rich and varied Alexander-tradition in western European literature. That honour belongs rather to the *Historia de preliis*, translated from the Greek in the middle of the tenth century in Naples by the Archipresbyter Leo at the behest of Duke John of Campania. The Greek version used by Leo was akin to that which, via Middle Persian and Syriac translations, gave rise to the extensive Alexander tradition of the Moslem world.

An example of romantic biography even more remote from reality and aiming at entertainment rather than instruction, is the *Ephemeris Belli Troiani*, 'Diary of the Trojan War', attributed to Dictys the Cretan, a companion on the Trojan campaign of Idomeneus and Meriones. Allegedly written in Phoenician characters, the work was said to have been discovered by Cretan shepherds in the age of Nero and transcribed into Greek. The Latin adaptation is the work of a certain L. Septimius and is dedicated to Q. Aradius Rufinus, who is probably to be identified with the consul of 311. The book recounts the story of the Trojan War from the Greek point of view from the seduction of Helen to the death of Odysseus, with much imaginative detail on the personal appearance of the heroes and such matters. A papyrus of A.D. 206 contains a portion of the original Greek Dictys, which Septimius appears to have translated fairly faithfully. The style is clear and simple, though monotonous. Occasional poetic or archaic expressions are designed to lend a patina of antiquity to the work. The ultimate source of Dictys, as of Dares Phrygius, is to be sought in Hellenistic treatises in which the post-Homeric treatment of Homeric themes, particularly by the Attic tragedians, was discussed. It was from Dictys and Dares that the western world in the Middle Ages learned what it knew of the Tale of Troy. The Greek east, although it had access to Homer, made much use of the lost Greek originals of Dictys and Dares, which are reflected in the *Antehomerica* and *Posthomerica* of John Tzetzes, the *Chronicle* of Constantine Manasses (both twelfth century) and the *Trojan War* of Constantine Hermoniakos (fourteenth century).

A similar account of the Trojan war from the Trojan point of view is attributed to Dares the Phrygian. It covers the period from the death of

Laomedon to the capture of Troy by the Greeks. A preface attributes the
Latin translation to Cornelius Nepos, who is said to have dedicated it to
Sallust. This is mere mystification. A date in the fifth or sixth century is sug-
gested by the language, which is less classical than that of Dictys. Like the
*Ephemeris* of Dictys, Dares' work is doubtless based on a Greek original,
but no trace of this has so far been found.

The history of Latin hagiography falls outside the scope of the present
volume, and the Lives of Saints written in the period under review can be dealt
with very briefly, with one important exception. Three main classical literary
genres contributed to the formation of the model followed by the typical
saint's life. These are the report of the trial and execution of the martyr, often
comprising authentic or spurious documents, the biography of the philosopher
or man of letters, and the account of the revelation of the superhuman powers
of the god in human guise or the man in a special relationship to the gods.
All three are found in various proportions in pagan texts such as the *Life of
Apollonius of Tyana* by Philostratus II and in certain of the *Lives of the Sophists*
by Eunapius. The Latin *Life of Cyprian* by his disciple Pontius, which survives
in a much interpolated form, still concentrates on the martyrdom of its subject,
and deals only with the last few years of his life. The *Life of Ambrose* by
pseudo-Paulinus and the *Life of Augustine* by Possidius remain much more
within classical patterns of biography. The three Lives of eastern monks
written by Jerome, those of Paul, Malchus and Hilarion, contain more elements
of aretalogy, as the miraculous ascetic feats of their subjects form the main
subject of the narration. The fascinating *Life of Martin of Tours* by Sulpicius
Severus combines a narrative of the exploits of its hero with the revelation
of his superhuman powers, culminating in his raising of a dead man to life.

There is little trace of Christian autobiography until the end of the fourth
century, though Jerome records a certain Aquilius Severus from Spain who died
in the reign of Valentinian and who wrote a work containing '*totius suae
uitae statum*' in prose and verse under the title Καταστροφή or Πεῖρα. This
work, which does not survive, may have been the first example of the specifically
Christian genre of 'inner' autobiography, in which a man recalls and examines
his own spiritual development. The first undoubted example of inner autobiography, a work which opens new paths in terms of ancient literary traditions
and which exercised immense influence on western European literature, is the
*Confessions* of Augustine. Augustine's role in the history of Christian thought
is a topic which does not fall within the scope of the present study. But it
would be impossible to discuss Latin literature in late antiquity without
dwelling on two of his principal works, the *Confessions*, which will be examined
here, and the *City of God*, which will be discussed in the context of the historiography of the late Empire.

The *Confessions*, in thirteen books, were written about 397, in the early years of Augustine's episcopate of Hippo. In form they are a dialogue between the author and God, or more strictly a monologue addressed by the author to God. The ancient reader on opening the work might well feel that what hé had before him was a philosophical treatise written in the form of a prayer, for which Plotinus himself, and even more his successors, provided a model. In content the first nine books recapitulate in chronological order the development of Augustine's spiritual understanding from his first infancy to the death of his mother Monnica in 387, dwelling in anxious detail on those episodes, often trivial in themselves, which marked an advance in the author's insight into his own nature and his place in the created universe. The last four books are a philosophical and theological analysis of the state of Augustine in particular and of man in general with reference to God and to the Christian church. The *Confessions*, however, are not a series of reminiscences. Though Augustine can project himself back into early manhood, youth and childhood with marvellous empathy, he is not interested in recreating a past which might otherwise be lost, or in telling a good story. What concerns him is how he, Augustine, came to be chosen by God for the gift of grace and what it implies. Yet is it not a story with a happy ending, as, in a sense, were the lives of the martyrs. At the end of it all Augustine recognizes that he has made progress. But his new state brings with it even more problems than his original innocence. Understanding brings a bleak and discouraging view of mankind, and little by way of comfort.

Augustine has a talent for narrative, and there are many brilliant narrative passages in the *Confessions*, such as the story of the boys stealing the pears in Carthage (2.4.9) or of Alypius, future lawyer and bishop, being arrested as a burglar (6.9.14). But a story is never told for its own sake. The brooding presence of the Bishop of Hippo is always there to comment, interpret, draw the lesson. In the numerous passages of direct address to God all the devices of ancient rhetoric are brought into play, as might be expected of the former holder of a chair in that subject. Augustine varies the pace and style of his long soliloquy with the skill expected of a successful professional. And he adds a new quality to his Latin prose by the continuous references, sometimes by verbatim quotation, sometimes by the most indirect allusion, to the Bible and in particular to the Psalms (naturally in a pre-Hieronyman version). This resulted not merely in adding a certain depth of meaning to what Augustine had to say, but also in the incorporation into artistic Latin prose of a whole exotic vocabulary and a strange universe of reference which had been hitherto spurned by men of classical learning, even if they were Christians.

This long account of the spiritual journey of a man brought up in the purest of classical tradition through Manichaeanism and Neoplatonism to a wholehearted commitment to a somewhat daunting Christianity is unique in Latin literature. Probably intended in the first place for the author's fellow-clerics and *servi Dei*, the book has enjoyed immense influence throughout a millennium and a half. To the reader sensitive to such matters it is a work which still touches the heart and mind with astonishing power. Others find the pervasive rhetoric cloying and dissuasive. To the student of the psychology of religion it is a document of deepest interest. Augustine himself, rereading his *Confessions* at the age of seventy-four, as the restless Berbers pressed even harder on the great Roman landlords of Africa, and as Gaiseric and his Vandals stood poised by the Straits of Gibraltar, observed 'they still move me when I read them now, as they moved me when I first wrote them' (*Retractationes* 2.32).

# 4

# HISTORY

After the death of Tacitus the Muse of history maintained virtual silence in the Latin west for two and a half centuries. This is partly to be explained by the role of history in Roman culture. Traditionally, the writing of history— the history of one's own times or of the immediately preceding age—had been an occupation for retired or failed statesmen, an aspect of their *otium* which corresponded to their political *negotium*. This meant that it was essentially an activity of senators. From Cato the Censor through Calpurnius Piso, Caesar, Sallust, Asinius Pollio, Cluvius Rufus to Tacitus the succession of senatorial historians stretches across the centuries. But by Tacitus' time there was no longer an independent political role for senators to play. They needed neither to proclaim their successes nor to justify their failures. The making of decisions had passed into other hands than theirs. They could only look back nostalgically and recount the successive stages by which they had lost their *libertas* (in the special sense which the word bore in senatorial thinking[1]). After Tacitus' time it was too late to do even that. The memory of *libertas* had perished. At the same time the composition of the senatorial class itself had changed. From being a small, close-knit, relatively exclusive group of central Italian landowning families, traditionally concentrating in their hands the exercise of the power of the Roman *res publica*, in spite of, or sometimes thanks to, the occasional maverick who appealed over the heads of his colleagues to the people of Rome, it had become a wide-open group of upper-class families from Italy and the western provinces, with little of the old solidarity or sense of destiny. As men from the eastern provinces, whose native tongue was Greek and who were heirs to a very different political tradition, began to enter the Senate in increasing numbers in the late second century, the complexion of the senatorial class became even more unlike what it had been in the later Republic or under the Julio-Claudian emperors. Thus the peculiarly Roman phenomenon of the senatorial historian, for whom history was an extension of politics, vanished with the social system which had given him birth.

[1] Cf. Wirszubski (1950) 124–71.

Not all Republican or early Imperial historians had been senators, of course. Some were probably clients of great senatorial houses, like Claudius Quadrigarius or Valerius Antias. Others were independent men of letters, pursuing no public career and owing allegiance to no patron. The greatest of these was Livy. Livy wrote at a time when men were sharply conscious of change. A historical epoch was coming to an end within his own lifetime. As his later books have perished we scarcely know with what thoughts and feelings he greeted the end of the Republic and the institution of autocratic rule – however much tempered by formal concessions to the authority of the Senate. But we can hardly suppose that the sense of radical change was absent from his mind as he wrote his rich, slow-moving nostalgic panorama of the history of the Roman people from Romulus to Augustus. That sense of change, of movement from one epoch to another, was no longer present in Roman society after the Julio-Claudians. However much things did in fact change, the changes were slow and almost imperceptible. They did not awaken in men's minds a sense of crisis and a need to re-examine the whole of their historic past. So Livy had no successors, only epitomators.

In the Greek world Clio was not silent. There the writing of history had different roots, going back to Polybius, Isocrates, Thucydides. Some of it was merely *belles-lettres*, designed to give pleasure or to move the emotions harmlessly. Much was concerned with understanding and edification. Much of it, such as the history of Polybius, had a political side to it – Polybius strove for pragmatic understanding of what had made Roman power, at a particular conjuncture in the history of the Mediterranean world, irresistible; what he was not concerned with, overtly at any rate, was the justification of his own conduct or that of a faction to which he belonged. This was a stance very different from, and much more 'intellectual' than that of the Roman senatorial historian. So Greek historiography was less dependent on the survival of a particular political and social structure than was that of the Roman world. In fact all the many strands of the rich Greek historical tradition continued to run through the 230 years after Tacitus, and there was a continuous and varied succession of historians writing in Greek on a variety of topics throughout the period.

In the second century Arrian of Nicomedia wrote not only a history of Alexander based on reliable contemporary sources, but also a whole series of local or provincial histories – *Bithynica, Parthica* etc. – and a history of the Greek world under the successors of Alexander; none of these last has survived. His contemporary Appian of Alexandria wrote twenty-four books of Roman history. Lucian's satirical *How to write history* reveals a dozen or more historians writing in a variety of styles – largely archaizing – on the Parthian war of Lucius Verus. In the first half of the third century Cassius Dio Cocceianus of Nicaea, consul in 223/4 and again in 229, devoted his retirement to writing a vast history of Rome from Aeneas to Severus Alexander in eighty books, much of which now survives only in excerpts or in an eleventh-century epitome. Derivative for the most part and displaying all the shortcomings of the rhetorical culture of the age, it is nevertheless a major work of synthesis, upon which the author has imposed the impress of his own personality and the political outlook of the senatorial class of his time. It is the first major history of Rome since Livy, and significantly it is written in Greek. In the same period Herodian, possibly a Syrian, wrote his history of the Roman world from the death of Marcus Aurelius in 180 to the accession of Gordian III in 238, a work much inferior in insight to that of Cassius Dio. Later in the century P. Herennius Dexippus of Athens wrote four books on Greece under the successors of Alexander, largely dependent on the work of Arrian, a universal chronicle from mythical times to the reign of Claudius Gothicus, and a history of Gothic wars up to at least 270. At the beginning of the fifth century Eunapius of Sardis wrote a continuation of the chronicle of Dexippus up to 404. As well as these major figures we hear of many other historians writing in Greek, some dealing with local or regional history, others with larger themes, like the apparently Roman Asinius Quadratus, who wrote a history of Rome from the foundation of the city to the reign of Severus Alexander in Ionic dialect in imitation of Herodotus.

In the same period Christians were beginning to write in Greek either on the history of the church or on universal history seen from the Christian point of view. Sextus Julius Africanus, an African philosopher turned Christian, wrote a history of the world from the creation to the reign of Macrinus (217–18) as well as a treatise on chronology in which Old Testament and Greek history were brought together. This in itself was a departure from the rhetorical tradition of classical historiography, which concerned itself only spasmodically and unsystematically with such matters. But the man who set a new stamp on Christian history-writing was Eusebius of Caesarea. Like Julius Africanus he was interested in tying together biblical history and the political history of the Graeco-Roman world, and to this end engaged in chronological researches, and published a world chronicle accompanied by comparative tables of dates, which does not survive in the Greek original. When he came to write the history of the Christian church from its beginnings to his own times in ten books he faced a new problem. The point of view which he expressed would be disputed not only by traditional pagans, but also by sectarian fellow-Christians. Neither would be likely to be convinced by rhetorical set-pieces, fictitious speeches, descriptive passages, general arguments, and the like, of which so much use had been made by the historians of the Roman empire, themselves the products of a rhetorical education and addressing themselves to a readership which shared their culture. What was needed was evidence, above all documentary evidence. So Eusebius turned his back on the literary approach of traditional historians and quoted his sources, together with the arguments for their authenticity, in his text. In so doing he was taking over for history the techniques and methods hitherto used exclusively by the antiquarian and the philologist, and restoring to it that concern for truth to which it had always laid claim but often forgotten in its preoccupation with matters of form.

This development began in the more lively world of Greek historiography and found for a time no echo in the Latin west, which produced scarcely any historical writing between the early second and the late fourth century.

Florus (pp. *The Early Principate*, pp. 168–9) wrote his summary of Roman history from the foundation of the city to Augustus in two books in the reign of Hadrian. Granius Licinianus' brief history of Rome, of which only a few fragments survive in a palimpsest manuscript, is probably to be dated in the same period, though some have argued for a date towards the end of the second century. When the surviving epitome of Livy was written – *T. Livi periochae omnium librorum ab urbe condita* – itself based on an earlier and longer résumé of Livy's immense history, is uncertain. It was used by Julius Obsequens for his collection of *prodigia* in the third or fourth century. We possess an epitome of the universal history – *Historiae Philippicae* – of Augustus' Gaulish contemporary Pompeius Trogus by M. Junianus Justinus. Nothing is known with certainty regarding his date. But it has been plausibly conjectured that he wrote some time in the third century. The relation of Justin's epitome to the lost work of Trogus is far from clear. It seems to consist of a mixture of excerpts and summaries, to have concentrated on what had exemplary value, and to have been written with students of rhetoric in mind. Thus most of the richness of Trogus' work, which depended largely on lost Greek sources, has been lost in the flat, sententious and awkward narrative of his epitomator. The best that can be said for Justin is that in a barbarous age he provided Latin readers with some insight, however distorted, into the wider world of Hellenistic historiography.

The political and economic stabilization of the empire begun under Diocletian and completed in the long reign of Constantine provided the foundation for a revival of culture in general and of literature in particular in the west in the fourth century. In the field of history the recovery was slow. There was no writing of history on the grand scale until the end of the century. And this renaissance of Latin historiography, like the rebirth of Latin poetry in the hands of Claudian, owed much to the Greek world, as will be seen. In the meantime the 60s and 70s saw the production of a series of epitomes or potted histories of Rome. Two of these – the *Breviaria* of Eutropius and of Festus – were written under imperial patronage; we know virtually nothing of the origins of the others. However they all seem to have answered the needs of a new ruling group, who had to be reminded of the past of the empire which they now administered, and at the same time to have served as vehicles for the political outlook of those who still remembered the Roman past, the Italian senatorial class and its dependants, now partly excluded from the key decision-making positions in the empire. One must beware of exaggerating the gulf which separated the two groups. Illiterate soldiers may briefly have held supreme power in the dark days of the third century. But the military establishment that surrounded Valentinian and Valens and which monopolized so many high offices of state did not consist of ignorant barbarians. Its members came in the main from the towns of the Danubian provinces, from Rhaetia to the Black Sea. Sons of middling landowners and members of small town councils, they had been to school, though few of them had gone on to study rhetoric. But their whole outlook was provincial and local and in particular non-Mediterranean, their experience military rather than political. What they lacked was a sense of the greatness of the Roman empire, of the stages through which it had passed, of the problems which its rulers had solved, of the dangers of regionalism and division. Similarly, the civilians who filled posts in the vast new bureaucracy created – or tolerated – by Diocletian and Constantine were not ignoramuses. They too were the sons of local worthies from the cities of Gaul, Spain, and Africa, men who had learned their Virgil at school as well as studying the shorthand which was now often the key to promotion. But they were provincials, their horizon limited by the boundaries of their city or their province. The ecumenical outlook of the old Roman Senate was strange to them. They had to be indoctrinated with it. They had to learn to surmount the narrow limits of space and time within which their political thinking had been confined, and draw long-term lessons from the contemplation of the more than millenary history of the Roman state. So, in broad outline, thought the authors of these fourth-century compendia of Roman history and their patrons. And each sought to meet the need in his own way.

Before coming to the surviving compendia, however, a word must be said about a fourth-century historical work which does not survive and which, in the view of some scholars, never existed. In 1884 E. Enmann argued at length that the numerous agreements between Aurelius Victor, Eutropius, and the *Historia Augusta* pointed to a common source, a narrative history of the Roman empire from the second to the end of the third century, which he dated in the reign of Diocletian. Subsequent studies suggest that a date shortly after the death of Constantine in 337 provides a better working hypothesis. This anonymous – and hypothetical – work of history is generally referred to as Enmann's *Kaisergeschichte*. Opinions vary as to its scale, but it is generally thought to have been a fairly brief chronicle in the style of Florus rather than a long and discursive history. Many scholars have denied its very existence, and they may well be right. But in general it is today accepted, but with caution. It appears to have contained detailed information on places and events on the Danubian frontier. The *Kaisergeschichte* maintains a ghostly existence just beyond our field of vision. There are however many historical compendia which still survive.

The earliest in date is that of Sextus Aurelius Victor. Born in Africa probably about 330 he was, he declares, of humble country stock. Perhaps he was the son of a small-town *curialis*, or of a *colonus* under the lex Manciana, who acquired quasi-ownership of waste land which he brought under cultivation. At any rate, like many men in the fourth century, he found literary skill a means of upward social mobility. He probably practised at the bar or entered the ranks of the civil service. He was in Sirmium when it surrendered to Julian in 361. He attracted the favourable notice of the emperor, who appointed him governor (*consularis*) of the province of Pannonia Secunda, corresponding roughly to present-day Serbia. He presumably fell from office, like most of Julian's appointees, after the emperor's death in 363. But he must have commended himself to subsequent emperors, as we find him holding the office of *iudex sacrarum cognitionum* under Theodosius, who in 389 appointed him to the prestigious dignity of Prefect of the City of Rome, an office usually held by senior members of the Senate. Thereafter he disappears from view. Ammianus Marcellinus, who was writing his history in Rome in 389 and who may well have known Victor personally, speaks with approval of his *sobrietas* (soundness, steadiness: 21.10.6). One would like to know more about a man who rose so high from such unpromising beginnings. Our only source of information is his résumé of the history of the Roman empire from Augustus to Constantine II in about fifty printed pages written, on internal evidence, in 360. It is generally known as the *Caesares*, though it bears other titles in some manuscripts. Though Julian probably knew of its existence, it was not composed at his behest or dedicated to him.

It is biographical in its approach, in the sense that Victor treats Roman history reign by reign and concentrates on the character and activities of each emperor. But he does make some attempt to surmount the limits of biography and to write history both by the inclusion of narrative passages and by the frequent moral and political judgements which he expresses, often in rather sententious fashion. His work is an example of that fusion of the methods of history and biography which was characteristic of the age.[1] Victor's method is not to give a balanced summary of the political and military events of each reign, but rather to pick on one or two episodes to the neglect of the rest. He tries not to present his characters in black and white, but to see both their

[1] Cf. Momigliano (1969) 286–303.

good and their bad points. His point of view is senatorial, as was that of almost all Roman historians, and he condemns strongly the exercise of state power by military men with military methods. For him the anarchy of the third century was a nightmare, the stabilization under Diocletian and above all under Constantine and his sons a restoration of proper government. But he blames the senatorial class for having let power slip from its hands through selfishness— *Dum oblectantur otio simulque diuitiis pauent, quarum usum affluentiamque aeternitate maius putant, muniuere militaribus et paene barbaris uiam in se ac posteros dominandi* 'Taking their pleasure in idleness and trembling for their riches, the enjoyment and abundance of which they looked on as more important than immortality, they [i.e. the senators] paved the way for soldiers and near barbarians to tyrannize over themselves and their descendants' (37.7). He attaches the highest value to literary culture, which can confer some dignity on even the meanest of rulers (43.8), and the lack of which abases even the noblest natural endownments (40.13). He is clearly a pagan, but avoids anti-Christian pronouncements. His style is jumpy and uneven, moving from well-structured and occasionally pompous rhetoric to loose anecdotal narrative. He mingles echoes of Sallustian terseness with the inflated verbosity of the administrative language of his age. His sources certainly included Suetonius and Marius Maximus. He probably also had before him lists of emperors with brief accounts of their reigns, like those put into verse by Ausonius. Whether he also consulted the hypothetical *Kaisergeschichte* is best regarded as an open question. The same holds good of recent suggestions that he knew the work of Tacitus. Whatever his sources, he made many stupid mistakes in using them. But his aim was a lofty one; he wanted to write a history of the Roman empire which combined interest in the character of individual emperors with an overall moral view of the empire. That he was not a Tacitus is scarcely to be held against him.

Aurelius Victor's compendium dealt only with the history of Rome since Augustus. At some time – probably in the fourth century or the beginning of the fifth, but some have conjectured a much later date – it was combined by an unknown editor with two other historical summaries to give a continuous history of Rome from the earliest times to the fourth century. The first of these, the *Origo gentis Romanae*, dealt with the legendary period from Saturn to Romulus. The second, *De viris illustribus urbis Romae*, covered the period of the monarchy and the Republic. Both works are of unknown authorship; they are manifestly not by the same hand. The *Origo gentis Romanae* was thought by Niebuhr to be a forgery by some Renaissance antiquarian. This it cannot be, as it is quoted by an early twelfth-century writer. It is now generally recognized to be a work of late antiquity, probably of the fourth century. In consequence of its subject matter it draws largely on Virgil and on his commentators. But it also contains many references to authorities of the Republican period and to others of whom nothing whatever is known. Its author has often been accused of falsification, but the charge must remain not proven. It cannot be excluded that this fourth-century scholar had access to a handbook of the Augustan age also used by Dionysius of Halicarnassus. The general tone of his exposition is rationalizing and euhemeristic, treating mythology as misunderstood history. The language and style are those of the fourth century, without the usually declamatory tone of voice, a language and style which suggest the grammarian rather then the rhetorician. The *Origo* is still something of an enigma, in spite of the vindication of its authenticity.

The *De viris illustribus* is a series of eighty-six biographies of leading men, beginning with Proca, king of Alba Longa, and Romulus, going on through the kings of Rome and the founding fathers of the Republic to the heroes of the early Republic like Camillus, P. Decius Mus and T. Manlius Torquatus, historical figures like Appius Claudius Caecus, Quintus Fabius Maximus Cunctator, Cato the Censor and Scipio Africanus, and concluding with the men of the last century of the Republic, the Gracchi, Marius, Saturninus, Sulla, Caesar, Cicero, Antony and Octavian. It includes biographies of a few enemies of Rome, such as King Pyrrhus of Epirus, King Antiochus of Syria, Mithridates, and Cleopatra, whose brief biography concludes the series. In its present form the work contains no preface and no narrative links between the biographies. The style at its best is crisp and epigrammatic, with a tendency to forced antitheses – Cleopatra *tantae libidinis fuit, ut saepe prostiterit, tantae pulchritudinis, ut multi noctem illius morte emerint* 'So great was her lust that she often prostituted herself, so great her beauty that many gave their lives for a night with her'. At its worst it is awkward and pretentious. The language is post-classical. The editor who compiled the corpus of Roman history believed that the *De viris illustribus* was an epitome of Livy. In fact the sources are, as might be expected in the case of a compendium of generally accessible information, not easy to identify. They may include Hyginus and Florus as well as some kind of Livian epitome. The *De viris illustribus* is useful in that it covers two gaps in the surviving epitome of Livy. None of the three works included in the corpus has any systematic chronological framework.

Of Eutropius all that is known with certainty is that he accompanied the emperor Julian on his Persian campaign and that he was private secretary (*magister memoriae*) to Valens, at whose behest he wrote his historical compendium in 369 or 370. He may well have been private secretary to all emperors from Constantius II to Valens. He is very probably to be identified with the Eutropius who was proconsul of Asia in 371–2, was accused of treason by his successor in office but acquitted, was Praetorian Prefect of Illyricum in 380–1, and consul along with Valentinian in 387. Thus he would be a senator who held a series of high offices over a long period of years. Whether he is to be identified with a Eutropius from Bordeaux who was interested in medicine is more than doubtful, as is also the statement in a tenth-century encyclopaedia that he was a teacher of rhetoric. His *Breviarium ab urbe condita* in ten books provides a survey of Roman history from the foundation of the city to the accession of Valens in 364. It is a conscientious, careful work, which seeks to provide information on the main events, particularly in the field of military and foreign affairs, without the capricious selectivity characteristic of Victor. Eutropius is precise, though not always correct, in matters of chronology, dating events not only by consulates, but by years from the foundation of the city, for which he accepts Varro's date of 753 B.C., and by the period which had elapsed since other important events. He gives countless names and figures. The scale of the *Breviarium*, and the author's limitations as a historian, preclude any serious analysis of historical causes. There are few, and very brief, descriptive passages, and fewer anecdotes than in the *De viris illustribus* or Aurelius Victor. Eutropius has no time for frivolity. His narrative is carefully structured, avoiding sudden jumps. The view of Roman history which he presents is conventional in his age. Collaboration between emperor and Senate, essential for the wellbeing of the state, was abruptly interrupted in 235 with the accession of the rude soldier Maximinus, and restored only under the family of Constantine. It is interesting, however, to note that Julius Caesar, a hero for Aurelius Victor, is a tyrant for Eutropius. He makes no mention of Christianity and was presumably a pagan. His style is smooth and lucid, if a trifle dry, without either far-fetched figures or lapses into formlessness. His sources are difficult to identify. They probably included an epitome of Livy, Florus, and the lost history of the empire written in the age of Constantine, if indeed it existed. While all the fourth-century epitomators are mediocre writers and poor historians, Eutropius is decidedly the best of them. His work enjoyed great popularity and was only partially replaced by the Christian compendium of Orosius in the fifth century. It was translated into Greek before the end of the fourth century by Paeanius or Paeonius, a pupil of Libanius, and again in the sixth century by the Lycian Capito, perhaps in connexion with Justinian's programme to bring the Latin west back under Roman rule. The former translation survives entire, the latter only in fragments.

Festus (his full name is unknown) was another self-made man, from Tridentum in Rhaetia, who rose to high rank through literary talent, practice at the bar, and marriage to a rich wife. In the later 60s he was governor (*consularis*) of Syria, where he tried to trap Libanius by accusing a friend of his of magical practices. Before the end of the decade he had become private secretary (*magister memoriae*) to Valens, probably in succession to Eutropius, and about 372 was appointed Proconsul of Asia. In this post he had the philosopher Maximus,

Julian's teacher and friend, executed. He was dismissed after the death of Valens in 378 and died of a stroke in the temple of Nemesis at Ephesus in 380. He is almost certainly the Festus who wrote the *Breviarium rerum gestarum populi Romani*, a very brief compendium of Roman history from the foundation of the city to the reign of Valens, written in 369 at the request of that emperor. It is much shorter than the *Breviarium* of Eutropius – about fifteen printed pages against about sixty – and somewhat differently arranged. There is no real chronological narrative of Republican history. The three Punic wars, which get fairly full treatment in three separate passages in Eutropius, are dismissed with the words *ter Africa rebellauit* 'thrice Africa revolted'. What Festus offers instead is a region by region account of the growth of the Roman empire. Similarly, the history of the empire is represented by a description of the wars on the eastern frontier waged by Pompey, Crassus, Augustus, Nero, Lucius Verus, Severus Alexander, Valerian, Aurelian, Diocletian, Constantine, Constantius II, Julian and Jovian. This concentration on Persian wars explains the genesis of the work. It is a piece of propaganda in connexion with Valens' planned campaign in the east, to which reference is made in the concluding words *etiam Babyloniae tibi palma pacis accedat* 'may the prize of pacifying Babylon too be granted to you'. Festus' text is so compressed that it can scarcely be said to have a style at all. His sources, as in all such cases, are hard to determine. Florus, an epitome of Livy fuller than that now surviving, Suetonius, Eutropius, and the putative history of the empire written under Constantine have been suggested. For the historian what is valuable in this jejune compendium is the list of dioceses and provinces in the reign of Valens and some of the details on the eastern wars of Aurelian and Diocletian.

The last of the fourth-century historical compendia has been handed down anonymously. The *Epitome de Caesaribus* is described in the two manuscripts in which it survives as being a résumé of the work of Aurelius Victor. It does indeed draw on Victor for material on the earlier emperors, but it is an independent work. It occupies about forty printed pages. In form it is a succession of brief imperial biographies, from Augustus to Theodosius, usually beginning with each emperor's birthplace, the length of his reign, and the principal events in it, and going on to a description of his personal appearance and character. The author is particularly interested in the details of his subjects' private life and above all in their sexual habits. The style is pompous, forced, and cliché-ridden, e.g. *stabant acerui montium similes, fluebat cruor fluminum modo* 'Piles of corpses stood high as mountains, blood flowed in rivers' (42.14). The author frequently draws on Eutropius. Many of the personal details come from Suetonius and doubtless from Marius Maximus. He may have used the supposed imperial history written in the age of Constantine, and it has been plausibly suggested that he also used the lost *Annales* of Nicomachus Flavianus.

59

His identity is likely to remain a mystery. He can hardly be an official of Theodosius' court, as he makes too many mistakes about the reign of that emperor. Perhaps he was a Roman senator or a member of his entourage. He could be the mysterious historian to whom Symmachus addressses *Epist.* 9.110, but this can be neither proved nor disproved. At any rate he was a pagan – he never mentions Christianity – and he identifies himself with pro-senatorial points of view. The *Epitome* must have been written shortly after Theodosius' death in 395. But to see in it a defence of the stance adopted by the pagan senators during the usurpation of Eugenius, as some scholars have done, is to force the evidence. The *Epitome* is riddled with errors, and any information for which it is the sole authority must be treated by the historian with circumspection.

There is no doubt of the anti-Christian sympathies of Virius Nicomachus Flavianus, one of the leaders of the Roman Senate in the closing decades of the fourth century. Governor (*consularis*) of Sicily, where his family owned estates near Henna in 364, he became successively *uicarius* of Africa (in 377), *quaestor sacri palatii* (in 389), and twice Praetorian Prefect (in 390 and 393). A militant pagan, who looked forward to the collapse of Christianity, he took the side of the pro-pagan usurper Eugenius in 393 and held the consulate under him in 394. After the defeat of Eugenius by Theodosius in that year he committed suicide. He translated from Greek Philostratus' *Life of Apollonius of Tyana*, which was seen in the fourth century as a pagan counterpart to the Christian gospels, and wrote a history of Rome, entitled *Annales*, which he dedicated to Theodosius. Neither work survives, and it is difficult to form a clear idea of the scope, scale and style of the *Annales*. Nicomachus Flavianus is treated by Symmachus with something like idolatry and is represented in the *Saturnalia* of Macrobius as a man of immense erudition, and is described in the inscription set up in the Forum during his consulship in 394 as '*historicus disertissimus*'. It would be rash to argue from this that his history must have been lengthy, penetrating and discursive. The circle of vastly rich senators to which he belonged were far too preoccupied with their own affairs to have deep insight into the political problems of the empire. As Nicomachus Flavianus himself writes in a letter to Symmachus (*Epist.* 2.34.2), *nihil hac aetate tractandum pensius domesticis rebus* 'these days nothing calls for greater attention than our private affairs'. His work is shown by its title to have been arranged annalistically, and in this point it is distinguished from the surviving compendia. It has sometimes been thought to have been used by Ammianus Marcellinus in his later books; the hypothesis is possible but undemonstrable. We have no reliable evidence on the period covered by the *Annales* of Nicomachus. The work may not have dealt with the author's own times.

There survives in a medieval florilegium a short history of the Roman empire under Constantine, which appears to be an excerpt from a longer work.[1] Crisp, clear and accurate, the extract makes no mention of Christianity – except in a few passages where verbatim excerpts from Orosius have been interpolated into the text – and the author may be taken to have been a pagan. Some have seen in this fragment a portion of the *Kaisergeschichte* of Enmann. At any rate it reminds us how much of the literature of late antiquity has perished and how provisional any judgements must be that are based on what chance and prejudice have preserved.

Roman historiography appeared to be degenerating into a series of jejune, derivative and superficial compendia, designed to remind a new ruling group of a tradition which they had forgotten or never learned, when suddenly towards the end of the fourth century a major historian, comparable with Sallust or Tacitus, appeared. Ammianus Marcellinus, though writing in Latin, was a Greek, familiar with the living tradition and practice of Greek historiography and welding it together with Roman gravity and sense of tradition to form a new whole. His situation can be compared to that of Claudian, who brought to the Latin west the skill and flexibility of contemporary Greek poetry, and successfully united it to Roman tradition to form a new, vigorous and viable poetic manner.

Ammianus Marcellinus was born in Antioch in Syria *c.* A.D. 325–30. He probably belonged to a family of *curiales* – wealthy city landowners whose members served on the city council. He would have the usual literary education of the upper-class youth in a great Greek city, studying classical literature and rhetoric. There is no reason to believe that he was ever a pupil of Libanius, though they knew one another in later life. His education completed, he took the unusual step of entering the army, perhaps as a means of escape from the increasing burdens falling on members of the curial class. He was enrolled in the *protectores domestici*, a corps recruited partly from experienced men from the ranks, partly from young men of good family, whose members acted as liaison officers and staff officers at the headquarters of commanders. From 353 or 354 he was attached to the staff of Ursicinus, the *magister equitum*, who was then in command of the Roman army on the Persian frontier, and remained with him for some seven years, travelling back from Mesopotamia through Antioch to Milan and on to Gaul and Cologne, then back via Sirmium to the east, again to Thrace, and back to Nisibis for Constantius II's campaign of 359. He took an active part in the fighting, was in Amida throughout its siege and capture by the Persians, and had several hair's-breadth escapes,

---

[1] Formerly attributed, along with an excerpt on Italy under Odovacar, to an Anonymus Valesianus (from Valesius, the Latin form of the name of the first editor Henri Valois), the work is now usually referred to as *Excerptum Valesianum* I. The other excerpt belongs to the work of a much later writer.

not all of which were to his credit. After the dismissal of Ursicinus in 360 we lose sight of Ammianus for several years, during which he presumably continued to perform his military duties. He is next found joining Julian's army at Cercusium for his ill-fated Persian campaign. After Julian's death and the disastrous failure of the campaign, Ammianus seems to have retired from the army – he had by now gained immunity from service in the *curia* – and to have devoted some years to study and travel. He certainly visited Egypt, ascending the Nile as far as the Thebaid, and was in Greece shortly after 366. He was in Antioch during the trials for magic and treason in 371, and may have been in some personal danger. It was during this period, probably quite soon after Julian's death, that he decided to write his history, and much of his study and travel was devoted to the collection of material for it. Some time after 378 he settled in Rome in order to complete his work. As a senior army officer, a man of letters and a wealthy man he would enjoy wide contacts there. But it is probably a mistake to suppose that he belonged to the circle of Symmachus, Nicomachus Flavianus and Praetextatus. These proud and self-centred aristocrats would probably have treated him as a kind of superior client, if they had deigned to notice him at all. On the other hand he is likely to have known the historian Eutropius, who had been with him in Julian's army in Persia, and he may well have known Aurelius Victor. He apparently gave readings of parts of his history as they were completed, and the news of the success of these reached distant Antioch, evoking a rather formal letter of congratulation from Libanius. Book 14 was written shortly after 383, Book 21 not earlier than 388–9, Book 22 by 391, and Book 31 possibly not until the death of Theodosius in 395. These dates give us a rough time-scale for the completion of the work. But Ammianus had clearly been occupied with it since the 60s of the fourth century. The date and manner of his death are unknown.

His history – *Res gestae* – in thirty-one books covered the period from the principate of Nerva to the death of Valens (96–378). Though Ammianus does not mention Tacitus, his choice of a starting point shows that he regarded himself as the continuator of Tacitus and implicitly dismisses all Latin histories since Tacitus as second-rate and unworthy. What survives are Books 14 to 31, dealing with the period 353 to 378. This leaves thirteen books to cover 257 years in the lost portion. Struck by the evident discrepancy in scale some scholars have suggested that Ammianus wrote two separate historical works, one in thirty-one books dealing with his own time, and one of unknown length recounting the previous two and a half centuries. But there is no trace of the alleged second work. And Ammianus' own references to his history of the early Principate are couched in exactly the same terms as those to earlier portions of the surviving text. It is likely that he dealt with the earlier period in more summary fashion, either by epitomizing, like the writers of compendia, or by selecting what he regarded as the most significant events, much as Procopius later prefaced to his history of the Persian wars of Justinian a survey of the military situation on the eastern frontier during the preceding century. Ammianus' method of work, as will be seen, was unsuitable for writing the history of the more distant past, for which he would have to depend on secondary sources. The question arises at what point detailed treatment began. The beginning of the surviving books, in the middle of the Caesarship of Gallus, is an unlikely point. Most probably Ammianus began his large-scale treatment with the death of Constantine in 337, but other hypotheses are possible.

Ammianus' subject is the history of the Roman empire, which for him comprised the greater part of the known world. He sees it against a larger but less distinct background, in which the ominous movements of peoples beyond the frontier can be discerned with greater or lesser clarity, while his curious eye on occasion ranges throughout the barbarian world, from the Attacotti, Scotti and Picti of northern Scotland (26.4.5, 20.1.1, 27.8.5) through the Goths (26.4.5, 27.4.1 etc.), the Sarmatians (26.10.20, 31.4.13), the Huns (31.2.1–2), the Sogdians (23.6.14) and the Indians (14.3.3, 23.6.12, 23.6.72–3, 31.2.16) to the distant Seres of China (14.3.3, 23.6.60–8, 31.2.15). His arrangement is chronological, but not strictly annalistic. His interest is no longer centred on court and Senate at Rome, with occasional glances at the activities of the frontier armies, as was that of Tacitus. The imperial court now moved from Trier to Milan, to Sirmium, to Constantinople, to Antioch. And sometimes the moment of decision was with the army rather than with the emperor. So Ammianus' scene shifts from Mesopotamia to Constantinople or Milan or Gaul, or even on occasion to Rome, as momentous events and decisions require. His canvas is far wider than that of Tacitus and the technical problems which he faces more complex. Indeed in Books 26 to 31, dealing with the period of Valentinian and Valens, the chronological sequence is virtually abandoned in favour of a geographical arrangement, as events in east and west follow their largely independent course.

The history of events is also the history of people. Ammianus' narrative is crowded with individuals, many of whom are introduced with a brief characterization: Orfitus is 'a man of prudence and a thoroughly experienced lawyer, but with a background in the liberal arts inadequate for a nobleman' (14.6.1), Viventius is ' a Pannonian, yet honest and prudent' (27.3.11). It is noteworthy that this treatment is reserved for civilians and that military men are never thus characterized. Some of the major figures receive somewhat longer and more formal descriptions, dealing with their physical appearance as well as their character, e.g. Gallus (14, 11, 27–78) or Procopius (26.6.1ff., 26.9.11). Petronius Probus, Praetorian Prefect in 368, head of the powerful Anician family, and clearly a man whom Ammianus detested, is honoured by a long and malicious character study (27.11.1–7). But it is above all the emperors whose appearance and character are described at length, often in formal set-pieces composed in accordance with the precepts of the rhetoricians: Julian (25.4.1–22), Jovian (21.6.4), Valentinian (30.7.1–30.9.6), Valens (31.14.1–9), Gratian (31.10.18–19), the usurper Silvanus (15.5.32–3). This interest in the personalities of rulers reflects the confusion of history and biography in late antiquity. There are only seventeen speeches in the surviving eighteen books, and most of these are addresses by emperors to their troops. Speeches in the Senate were no longer of significance. That the existing speeches are in general constructed in accordance with the handbooks does not mean that they are not true to life. Generals haranguing their soldiers rarely express original ideas.

The descriptions of military operations, of which there are many, are usually clear when Ammianus speaks as an eye-witness, but often obscure when he relies on the evidence of others. His unwillingness, in accordance with the precepts of rhetoric, to use technical terms often contributes to the obscurity of such passages. He owes little to the emotion-charged style of the traditional 'battle-piece', the roots of which go back to the pupils of Isocrates.

There are many digressions, usually formally marked as such, dealing with geography and ethnology, with physical matters such as earthquakes, eclipses, comets or the origin of pearls, with philosophical or religious topics like fate, prophecy or tutelary deities, and with aspects of the society of his time, such as life in Rome, the moral corruption of Roman society, or the shortcomings of lawyers. Many of those excursuses are explicitly intended to provide background to Ammianus' narrative: examples are those on the city of Amida (18.9.1–4), on Thrace and the regions bordering the Black Sea (22.8.1–48), on the history, geography and demography of the Persian empire (23.6.1–88), and on the Huns (31.2.1–12). Other digressions of the same type were evidently intended to provide similar background information. Others, like the long moralizing note on the decadence of Roman society (14.6.2–26) were connected with the author's overall view of the process of Roman history. Many of the scientific digressions were from the point of view of the ancient reader legitimate comment on the events narrated. They were also a display of the author's wide knowledge. Ammianus had read a great deal, was in his rather disorganized way a learned man, and had a deep respect for erudition in others. The next group of digressions, such as those on Egyptian hieroglyphic writing (17.4.1–23), on foreknowledge and augury (21.1.8–14), on the tragedian Phrynichus (28.1.3–4), are best understood as gratuitous displays of erudition which would give pleasure to like-minded readers. Finally there are those which are expressions of the author's own experience and judgement, such as that on the Roman nobility (28.4.6) or that on the legal profession (30.4.3–22). Occasionally we can hazard a guess at the sources used by Ammianus in his excursuses; in most cases they are unknown to us, but bear witness to the omnivorous character of his reading during the long years of gestation of the *Res gestae*.

Ammianus knew much more than he put down in his history. Again and again he dismisses certain topics as too trivial to record – anecdotes about emperors, the tittle-tattle of Roman aristocracy, minor details of campaigns, matters on which there is no agreement among authorities, and *quae per squalidas transiere personas* 'the exploits of humble individuals' (28.1.15). The reader is constantly reminded of the presence of the historian, selecting, rejecting and ordering his information in accordance with his conception of the dignity of history.

Ammianus was evidently a pagan. But he viewed with detachment verging on contempt the traditional Roman state religion. He is well informed on the organization and doctrine of the Christian church and freely uses some of its technical language. His attitude towards Christianity is on the whole detached and objective. But he can be scathing on the sectarian rivalries of the Christians and on the widening gap between profession and practice as Christianity spread among the upper classes of the empire (27.3.12–15). His own religious and philosophical views are never set out clearly. Perhaps they were not very clear. He was a monotheist, but in his explanation of human affairs he oscillates between providentialism and determinism, and at the same time leaves room for the *uirtus* of great men to determine the outcome of events. The background of his thought is probably the kind of second-hand Neoplatonism current in intellectual circles in the Greek east, its vagueness and confusion typical of the uncommitted and unphilosophical.

Ammianus was a patriot. For him the Roman empire was a universal and permanent state. Barbarians, though individually sometimes winning his respect, were in general objects of his contempt. Rome itself is *urbs aeterna*, 'the eternal city', *urbs sacratissima* 'the most sacred city', *templum mundi totius* 'the temple of the whole world', *imperii uirtutumque omnium lar* 'the domicile of empire and of every virtue', *caput mundi* 'the head of the world'. These terms refer to Rome as a political concept. The city itself still filled him with admiration, but its inhabitants – the fickle and greedy mob and haughty, idle and ignorant aristocrats – inspired his deepest misgivings. This discrepancy between the ideal and the real was a symptom of the crisis through which the empire was passing. That it was in crisis was not a matter of doubt. He comments sadly, if a little inaccurately, that Jovian was the first man in history to diminish the territory of the empire (25.9.9). Corruption and civil strife spread within the empire, as the rulers and their friends preferred personal advantage to honour (30.4.1). The ominous gathering of barbarian forces on the frontier led to the terrible climax of Adrianople, when a Roman army was destroyed and an emperor slain in battle. On every hand the clouds were gathering. What the nature of the crisis was remained vague. The quantifying methods of the economic or social historian were not available to Ammianus, or to any other historian of antiquity. Their approach was a moral one. The decadence and corruption of individuals and institutions was for them a sufficient explanation. Ammianus could not conceive of the fall of the Roman empire. But he was agonizingly aware of its decline, and this is the grand theme of his history.

His hero is Julian, whom he must have known personally. Julian's reign is recounted in detail in Books 16–25, his wisdom and the soundness of his policy are emphasized – though not without reserve – and the long obituary notice of him (25.4) makes it clear that for Ammianus his qualities far outshone those of any other ruler of his age – *uir heroicis paene connumerandus ingeniis*, 'a man to be numbered almost among the characters of legend'. Those passages were written a quarter of a century after Julian's death, the fruit of long study and reflection. Even in his old age Ammianus was haunted by the thought that had Julian lived, the squalor and disaster of succeeding years might have been avoided. In this sense there is a tragic colouring to Ammianus' view of Roman history. It was a tragedy of lost opportunity

Discussion of Ammianus' sources was a favourite occupation of nineteenth-century scholars. Today the matter can be dealt with briefly. There was no continuous narrative source on any scale available to Ammianus for the period covered by the surviving books. He made extensive use of documents – diplomatic and official correspondence, laws and edicts, speeches of emperors, and the like – to which his position must have given him easy access. Such sources he evidently sought out in public archives. He read Aurelius Victor, and probably Eutropius, and he may well have had other compendia at his disposal. But apart from documents his main sources were his own observation and the critical examination of witnesses – *ea quae uidere licuit per aetatem, uel perplexe interrogando uersatos in medio scire* 'what I could see myself because of my age, or what I could learn by careful interrogation of participants' (15.1.1). This is the method of Thucydides rather than that of Tacitus. That Ammianus can sometimes be shown to have got things wrong is no argument against the validity of his method.

Ammianus' native language was Greek. He probably learned Latin in his native Antioch – Libanius inveighs against the growing interest in the language of court, army and law – and he certainly used it daily throughout his army service. In his retirement, if not before, he read much classical Latin literature. His Latin has a Greek tinge to it, particularly in the frequency of participial phrases, and perhaps also in his sometimes odd word-order. But it is not, as some scholars used to suggest, a kind of translationese. He combines the freedom to form new words and the verbose style of official Latin of his own day with an eagerness to stud his text with archaic and poetic words and classical flosculi, in particular from Virgil. His training in rhetoric is responsible for his frequent and startling metaphors, such as *orientis fortuna periculorum terribilis tubas inflabat* 'the destiny of the East sounded the fearsome trumpet-blast of danger' (18.4.1) or *tempore quo primis auspiciis in mundanum fulgorem surgeret uictura dum erunt homines Roma* 'at the time when Rome, destined to live as long as mankind exists, was first beginning to rise to world-wide splendour' (14.6.3). He takes great pains to vary his expression in accordance with the precepts of rhetoric; his description of oil-wells in Assyria (23.6.17–18), too long to quote, is a palmary example, verging almost on caricature. Yet at the same time he makes use of a number of recurring clichés, like *supra modum*. He observes stress accent as well as quantitative metre in his clausulae. His style, though clearly belonging to the age in which he wrote, is highly personal and idiosyncratic. It is not compressed and suggestive, like that of Tacitus, and there are few well-constructed periods. Ammianus' sentences are long and rambling, and over-filled with qualifications, some of which in their turn form the nucleus of a string of subordinate clauses.

At the conclusion of his *Res gestae* Ammianus reminds his readers that he writes *ut miles quondam et Graecus* 'as a former soldier and a Greek' (31.16.9) the history of the Roman empire. The phrase is chosen for its paradoxical suggestions – a man of Greek culture writing Roman history, a member of the military profession – from which senators were excluded – engaging in a traditionally senatorial activity, a man from the Greek world of cities and peace practising the martial arts of Rome. All these points serve to underline the uniqueness of Ammianus and the grandeur of his achievement. A Greek soldier, he was the last of the great Roman historians.

History henceforth belonged to the Christians. Their purposes were in general different from those which had inspired Roman historians from Fabius Pictor to Ammianus Marcellinus. Christian Latin literature as such falls outside the scope of the present study. But a brief glance at some of the Christian works of history written in Latin in the two generations after the death of Theodosius will help to make clear the interplay of tradition and innovation in historical thinking as the western Roman empire crumbled away.

Jerome (340/50–419/20) was a writer of wide-ranging interests and activities, and his historical writings are not among his most important works. But they deserve mention in the present context. As Christianity made headway among the educated upper classes of the Latin world, they found themselves faced with the fact that Greek Christian literature was so much richer and more varied than their own. In particular thanks to Eusebius of Caesarea, who built on the foundations laid by Julius Africanus, the Greeks possessed an authoritative survey of world history from the Christian point of view, based on a firm chronology, and uniting Graeco-Roman history, biblical history, and the miscellaneous information on oriental history which the Greek world had acquired since the days of Alexander the Great. During his stay in Constantinople Jerome decided to translate and adapt the second book of Eusebius' *Chronicle*, consisting largely of tables of chronological concordance. To make this more attractive to the Latin reader of his own day he added material from Roman history, largely taken from Eutropius, from Suetonius' *De viris illustribus*, and from Roman lists of magistrates, and added a final section carrying on the *Chronicle* from 325 till 378. The adaptation was made, as Jerome himself tells us, in great haste. And though he displays his usual care for elegant writing, including the observation of metrical clausulae, there are many errors and signs of carelessness. The section which Jerome himself added is full of factual information, but its judgements are marked by his usual violent prejudices and his tendency to exaggerate the importance of his own circle of friends. Yet the *Chronicle* answered a need and enjoyed immense popularity during the author's lifetime and for many centuries afterwards.

Twelve years later, in 392, when he was established in his monastery at Bethlehem Jerome wrote his second historical work, which answered a similar need. Though Christianity was now firmly established as the state religion it was still open to the charge that its literature was poor in quality and quantity in comparison with that of paganism. As the devil has all the best tunes, so then he had all the best books. At the prompting of Nummius Aemilius Dexter, son of a bishop of Barcelona, who had already been proconsul of Asia and *comes rerum priuatarum*, and who was to be Praetorian Prefect of Italy in the last year of Theodosius' reign, Jerome compiled his *De viris illustribus*, a collection of 135 notes on Christian writers, both Greek and Latin, beginning with Peter and ending with Jerome himself. Most of the information came from Eusebius' *Ecclesiastical History*. But Jerome added much contemporary and Latin material from his own reading. To make up his number he includes not only Jews and heretics – a point for which Augustine censured him – but also Seneca, on the basis of his spurious correspondence with St Paul. This first manual of patrology is written in a simple and unadorned style. Like the *Chronicle* it betrays by its errors and confusion the haste with which it was written. Yet it remains a precious source of information. And, as with so much that Jerome wrote, it was a pioneering work, breaking new ground. It was translated into Greek in the early Middle Ages.

The richness of Greek Christian literature prompted the many translations made by Tyrannius Rufinus of Concordia near Aquileia, friend and later enemy of Jerome. He went to the east in the company of the elder Melania in 371, founded a monastery in Jerusalem and remained there until his return to Aquileia in 397. From then until his death in 410 he was mainly engaged in translating works of the Greek Fathers, particularly Origen, Basil and Gregory of Nazianzus. Most of these, as well as the polemical works which he wrote during his sojourn in Palestine, fall outside the scope of the present study. His *Ecclesiastical History*, however, calls for some notice. Rufinus was induced some time in the first decade of the fifth century by Chromatius bishop of Aquileia to translate the *Ecclesiastical History* of Eusebius, as nothing comparable existed in Latin. He abbreviated his original text, omitted many of the documents which it cited, and added two books of his own covering the period from 324 to 395. The translation is very free, and the style simple and unrhetorical, as befitted what was in essence a technical work. The two final books are based on Rufinus' own recollections and on the writings of the fourth-century church Fathers. In careful scrutiny of sources and critical acumen Rufinus falls short of Eusebius. He did however introduce a new genre into Latin literature.

About the same time or shortly afterwards Sulpicius Severus, a member of the cultivated Gaulish aristocracy, educated at Bordeaux and a friend of Paulinus of Nola, wrote a briefer but in some ways more original Christian history. His *Chronicle*, in two books, covers the period from the creation to A.D. 400, and is mainly devoted to biblical and church history. Sulpicius was a man of scholarly habits, with a feeling for the importance to the historian of documents. Inevitably he turned to Eusebius for much of his material. But he also drew on pagan historians and on his own very wide general reading. As befits the fellow-countryman, and perhaps even the pupil, of Ausonius, he writes clear, classical Latin. But his style is rather flat and undistinguished, without the panache which Jerome succeeded in displaying even in writing dry catalogues. He furnishes much useful information on events of his own lifetime.

On 24 August 410 the troops of Alaric the Visigoth captured and pillaged Rome. The Goths remained in the city only three days. The damage and loss of life were by ancient standards fairly light. Many of the better-off citizens had long ago left the city and taken refuge in Sicily, Africa or the east. Yet the reaction to the sack of Rome was out of all proportion to its real importance. The impossible had happened, and men could no longer be sure of anything. In far-off Bethlehem Jerome could no longer work on his Commentary on Ezekiel. *Quis crederet*, he exclaims, *ut totius orbis exstructa uictoriis Roma corrueret?* 'Who could believe that Rome, built upon victories over the whole world, could collapse?' (*In Ezech.* prol. in lib. 3, *PL* 25.75D). In a letter written at the same time he asks *Quid saluum est, si Roma perit?* 'What is safe, if Rome perishes?' (*Epist.* 123.16). Augustine's changing reaction to the catastrophic event can be traced in the sermons which he preached in 410 to 412 to his congregation in Hippo, which included many émigrés from Italy. He began by counselling asceticism, a *passe-partout* response to any difficult situation. But soon he turned to examining the grounds for the belief in the universality and eternity of the Roman empire. 'Heaven and earth will pass away, according to the Gospel, and if Virgil claims the contrary, it is purely from flattery. The poet well knew that all empires are perishable' (*Serm.* 105.7.10). His definitive response to the sack of Rome was his *magnum opus et arduum* the *De civitate Dei*, of which Books 1–5 were published in 413, Books 6–10 in 415, Books 11–13 in 417, Books 14–16 in 418, Book 17 in 420, and Books 18–22 not until 425. Full discussion of this remarkable work is inappropriate to the present context. But a brief treatment of Augustine's attitude to and use of Roman history is called for.

Alaric's capture of Rome provoked attacks on the position of the Christian church both by pagans and by Christians or former Christians. The pagans claimed that the recent disasters were due to the cessation of the worship of the old gods, and alleged by way of proof that things had been much better in the old days. The Christians complained that the fall of the city cast doubt upon the providential role of the Roman empire, in which men had come to believe more and more since the days of Constantine. Events also put in trenchant form the old problems of why the innocent suffered and the guilty were spared. Both these lines of attack were pursued at two levels. The man in the street thoughtlessly blamed the Christians for everything: *Pluuia defit, causa Christiani* 'There is not enough rain, the Christians are to blame' (Aug. *Civ. Dei* 2.3). *Multi, praeter-itarum rerum ignari ... si temporibus Christianis aliquod bellum paulo diutius trahi uident, ilico in nostram religionem proteruissime insiliunt* 'Many who are ignorant of history ... if they see some war drag on rather too long in the Christian age, at once impudently attack our religion' (Aug. *Civ. Dei* 5.22). *Si reciperet circum, nihil esse sibi factum* 'If the circus reopened, nothing would have happened to us' (Oros. 1.6.4). At another level the Neoplatonizing pagan scholars, the men for whom Macrobius wrote his *Saturnalia*, opposed to the historicism of Christianity an unchanging and eternal universe and a sophisti-cated and subtle theory of the position in it of man in general, and Roman man in particular. It was above all to the pagan cultivated upper classes that Augustine addressed himself in the *De civitate Dei*. His object was to provide an intellectual foundation for Christianity which would withstand their criticism and win their assent. At the same time he also sought to make some kind of reply to the more popular complaints. In the course of both these endeavours he sought to demythologize the idealized Roman past which both groups believed in, and into which the pagan intellectuals were wont to retreat as an escape from the harsh reality of their own times. This he did by demonstrating: (1) that Roman history is not full of moral *exempla*, (2) that disaster was as frequent and grave in the past as in the present, (3) that it was a symptom of human sinfulness, and had nothing to do with the virtues or vices of the Romans, who were no better or no worse than any other people, (4) that the Roman empire, while like all else the object of divine providence, was not essential for the salvation of man-kind, but that it was a historical phenomenon which would some time pass away.

All these points demanded constant historical illustration and historical discussion. And the readership to which Augustine addressed himself, so different from his down-to-earth congregation at Hippo, was accustomed to thinking in terms of Roman history. So the *De civitate Dei*, and especially the earlier books, is full of long polemical treatments of topics from the history of Rome and particularly of the Roman Republic, in which Augustine gave proof of his wide reading in the classical historians as well as in the recent epitomators. He examines the whole tradition of Roman history in a new light and subjects it to a new critique. Virgil had defined Rome's imperial mission as *parcere subiectis et debellare superbos* 'spare the submissive and conquer the proud' (*Aen.* 6.853). Augustine observes *Inferre autem bella finitimis et in cetera inde procedere ac populos sibi non molestos sola regni cupiditate conterere et subdere, quid aliud quam grande latrocinium nominandum est?* 'But to make war on one's neighbours, to go on then to others, to crush and subject nations who do us no harm out of mere greed for power, what else can we call that but brigandage on the grand scale?' (*Civ. Dei* 4–6).

At the same time his purpose went far beyond refuting erroneous ideas about the Roman past, and he began to resent the time spent in seeking out, analysing and refuting historical exempla. *Si narrare uel commemorare conemur*, he complains, *nihil aliud quam scriptores etiam nos erimus historiae* 'If I try to recount or mention [all those events] I too will be nothing but a historian' (*Civ. Dei* 3.18), *Si haec atque huiusmodi*, he asks, *quae habet historia, unde possem colligere uoluissem, quando finissem?* 'If I had wanted to gather together from where I could these and suchlike historical matters, when would I have finished my work?' (*Civ. Dei* 4.2). He was therefore glad to be able to entrust to a young Spanish priest called Orosius, who had come to visit him in Africa, the task of compiling a historical dossier as a kind of appendix to the early books of the *De civitate Dei*.

Orosius (the name Paulus is first attested by Jordanes in the sixth century and is of doubtful authenticity) was born in the Spanish provinces, probably at Bracara (now Braga in northern Portugal) about 375–80. About 410–12 he came to Hippo, either on a personal visit or as the delegate of the Spanish clergy. Augustine was impressed with his ability and willingness, and invited him to write a study of Roman history which would refute the criticisms both of pagans and of Christians. In 415 he sent him to Jerome in Bethlehem with a warm letter of introduction. In the same year Orosius took part in a local synod at Jerusalem, where he was the spokesman of the anti-Pelagians. By 416 he was back in Africa, where he remained until later 417 or 418. Thereafter all trace of him is lost. During this second stay in Africa he put the finishing touches to his *Historiarum adversus paganos libri VII*. This was committed history, written to prove a point. In it Orosius surveys the history of the world from the creation

until his own time using as a framework the concept of four successive empires –
Babylonian, Macedonian, Carthaginian and Roman. His praiseworthy attempt
to write universal rather than Roman history soon peters out, and the bulk of
the work is concerned exclusively with the history of Rome. The treatment
is highly selective, as Orosius' aim was to emphasize the grimness and
unpleasantness of life in pagan times. So bloody battles, earthquakes, famines
and plagues are described at length, while Rome's civilizing and pacifying
mission is constantly minimized. Orosius continually interrupts his narrative
to make personal comments, moral or ironical, on the matter which he
narrates, and to suggest to his reader the appropriate reaction. His apologetic
purpose leaves no room for the detached objectivity – real or feigned – of the
classical historian. So too his style owes little to traditional aesthetic theory. He
writes a Latin which is usually clear, vigorous and vivid, though sometimes
clumsy, with little use of rhetorical figures and of such traditional features of
historical narrative as the historic infinitive or the set speech. It is the language
of natural eloquence rather than that of the schools. He names many sources,
such as Plato, Polybius and Fabius Pictor, whom he cannot have read since he
knew no Greek. And many of the Latin sources which he mentions, like
Pompeius Trogus, Valerius Antias, or the emperor Claudius, he is unlikely to
have read. His true sources he mentions rarely or not at all. They are Justin,
from whom he gets most of his non-Roman history, Florus, Eutropius, Jerome's
*Chronicle*, perhaps the first five books of Augustine's *De civitate Dei*, Arnobius,
Sulpicius Severus. He may well have read Tacitus, and he had probably read
Sallust, who was a school author. Among poets he quotes Virgil and Lucan
whom he will have studied at school, and surprisingly enough Claudian (*De
III Cons. Honorii* 96–8, quoted at 7.35.21).

Orosius' highly partial survey of Roman history corresponds only to a part
of Augustine's purpose in the *De civitate Dei*, that of replying to popular claims
that everything had been better in the good old days and of undermining belief
in an idealized Roman past. He does not attempt to meet the philosophical
objections of the cultivated Neoplatonizing intellectuals, which is the principal
task that Augustine sets himself. His survey is hasty and not infrequently
muddled. But its simple style, its apologetic purpose and its clear message made
its fortune. It became the handbook of history *par excellence* in the Middle Ages,
used and excerpted by writers from Jordanes and Gregory of Tours to the eve
of the Renaissance. A translation into Old English was made on the orders of
King Alfred in the ninth century. In 1059 the Byzantine emperor Romanus II
sent a copy to the Caliph of Cordoba 'Abd ul-Rahmân III, who had it translated
into Arabic. It was one of the first classical texts to be printed (Augsburg 1471).

# 5

# ORATORY AND EPISTOLOGRAPHY

The study of rhetoric and the practice of declamation went on throughout the half-century of military anarchy in the third century. And though the occasions for great speeches in the Senate on matters of high policy were doubtless fewer than in the days of Pliny and Tacitus, debates continued. Some of them are recorded, however unreliably, in the *Historia Augusta*. It may be that one type of oratory even became more frequent. Roman emperors had always spent a surprising proportion of their time listening to speeches made by representatives of the Senate and delegates of provinces and cities. The only weapon which the senatorial class and the provincial upper classes could use to defend their position against their unpredictable and usually short-lived overlords was eloquence. We may be sure that they used it, even though none of their loyal addresses has been preserved. The stabilization effected by Diocletian and Constantine, with its concentration of the power of decision in the imperial court, resulted in the address to a ruler becoming almost the sole form of genuine public oratory, as opposed to mere declamation. From the fourth century we have a number of surviving speeches, all of which take the form of addresses to emperors. Whatever their ultimate purposes, such addresses inevitably struck a panegyric note.

But before going on to examine these surviving speeches, it would be well to glance at the material for the teaching of rhetoric produced during the period. It is in no sense literature, yet it must have exercised some influence on the oratory of its time. A number of such works survive, not so much because of their own qualities as because nothing better was ever written to replace them. Some deal with particular branches of rhetoric. An example is the *De figuris sententiarum et elocutionis* 'On figures of thought and speech' of Aquila Romanus, probably written in the third century, and completed by Julius Rufinianus in a work of the same title dating probably from the fourth century. Two short works, *De schematis lexeos* 'On figures of speech' and *De schematis dianoeas* 'On figures of thought' are also attributed in the manuscripts to Rufinianus. Aquila Romanus takes most of his illustrations of figures of rhetoric from Cicero, Rufinianus draws largely on Virgil. An undatable work

73

of late antiquity, the *Carmen de figuris* 'Poem on figures of speech', treats the same subject matter in verse as an aid to memory. Three hexameters are given to each figure, generally one for definition and two for illustration. Many of the examples are drawn from classical Greek and Latin writers, adapted in form to the needs of metre.

Other works on rhetoric are text-books covering the whole subject. They are impossible to date with certainty, as they never refer to contemporary events. Among such manuals are the *Ars rhetorica* of C. Julius Victor, which is based almost entirely on Quintilian, the *Institutiones oratoriae* 'Principles of oratory' of Sulpicius Victor, who claims to follow a certain Zeno (probably Zeno of Athens, whose manual of rhetoric in ten books does not survive), and the *Artis rhetoricae libri III* of C. Chirius Fortunatianus, arranged in the form of question and answer and drawing its doctrine from Quintilian and its illustrations from Cicero. The *Praecepta artis rhetoricae* 'Precepts of the art of rhetoric' of Julius Severianus, which claims to meet the needs of the practising advocate and which draws all its examples from Cicero, has been variously dated from the second to the fifth century. A fragment is preserved of Augustine's *De rhetorica*, which formed part of his handbook of the liberal arts (Halm 137–51). Augustine himself had lost most of this handbook by the time he came to write his *Retractationes* about 427.

What is striking about all these works, apart from their lack of originality, is the almost total absence of any Greek influence. The theory of rhetoric had not stood still in the Greek world. Hermogenes, the erstwhile infant prodigy turned teacher, wrote at the end of the second century a series of text-books of rhetoric which because of their orderly arrangement and their clarity of expression became standard works, commented upon endlessly by Greek school-masters up to the fifteenth century. Following in the wake of Hermogenes, Menander of Laodicea in Phrygia wrote in the third century a treatise on epideictic oratory, clear in exposition, copiously illustrated, and answering the needs of the age. (It survives in two versions, one of which may not be the work of Menander himself.) In the fourth century Aphthonius of Antioch wrote a manual of graded preliminary exercises (*Progymnasmata*) which partly replaced those of Hermogenes. And early in the fifth century Nicolaus of Myra in Lycia wrote a similar manual of *Progymnasmata*, which, like that of Aphthonius, was used and commented on by teachers in the Greek world throughout the Middle Ages. Of all this pedagogical literature, which introduced new distinctions and new methods of study, there is virtually no trace in the surviving Latin manuals of the fourth and fifth centuries. Quintilian is still their model, whether at first or second hand, and Cicero provides most of their illustrative material. They concentrate on deliberative and forensic oratory, for which there was little room in late antiquity, and have little to say about the panegyric and other forms of epideictic eloquence. Even in the humble sphere of the rhetorical school the division between Greek east and Latin west is clearly visible. It is worth recalling that Augustine, who taught rhetoric at Carthage and Milan, had little knowledge of Greek and depended on translations. The rhetoric of the fourth-century west owed nothing to the world of Libanius, Themistius and Himerius.

Some time towards the end of the fourth century a collection of twelve addresses to emperors dating mainly from the end of the third century and the first two thirds of the fourth was compiled, probably by a teacher of rhetoric and perhaps in Gaul. The collection is conventionally known as the *Panegyrici Latini*; there is no general title in the manuscripts. It begins with the Panegyric addressed to Trajan by the younger Pliny on the occasion of his consulship in A.D. 100, which is evidently regarded as a model for such compositions. The rest comprises eleven panegyrics delivered by persons having some connexion with Gaul. Mamertinus, a Gallic teacher of rhetoric, possibly from Trier, addresses two speeches to Maximian, one in 289 and the other probably in 291 (Nos. 2 and 3). Both were delivered in Trier. Eumenius, a rhetor from Autun and later – perhaps as a result of his speech – *magister memoriae* to Constantius Caesar in Gaul, delivered in 298 a speech of thanks for his appointment by Constantius as professor of rhetoric and organizer of the city schools in his native town, after it had been sacked by the Bagaudae (No. 4). Nazarius, a rhetor from Bordeaux, pronounced a panegyric on Constantine – in his absence – in 321 (No. 10). It was probably delivered somewhere in Gaul. Claudius Mamertinus, a man of probably Gaulish origin who rose to high office under Julian and held the consulship in 362, delivered an address of thanks to the emperor in Constantinople at the beginning of the year (No. 11). Latinius Pacatus Drepanius, a Gaul from near Bordeaux who was also something of a poet, delivered a panegyric on Theodosius in 389 in celebration of his defeat of Maximus (No. 12). It is no accident that he was appointed proconsul of Africa in 390 and *comes rerum priuatarum* in 393. The remaining speeches are transmitted anonymously. One, probably delivered in Trier in 297, is an address on behalf of the *ciuitas Aeduorum* (Autun) to Constantius Caesar, which dwells in particular on his recovery of Britain from the usurper Allectus (No. 5). A second was delivered in 307 on the occasion of the marriage of Constantine and Fausta, the daughter of Maximian (No. 6). It treats with coy reserve the abdication of Maximian, which everyone knew was forced upon him by Diocletian. The third was delivered in Trier in 310 by an orator from Autun in the presence of Constantine, who is congratulated on his victory over his father-in-law Maximian (No. 7). The fourth, a speech of thanks on behalf of the citizens of Autun, was delivered in 312 in Trier in the presence of Constantine (No. 8). The fifth was delivered in a Gaulish city, probably Trier, in 313 to congratulate Constantine on his victory over Maxentius (No. 9). Some of these anonymous speeches are probably by Eumenius, the author of No. 4, but proof is impossible. There is great similarity in style and arrangement between all the speeches. All of them strike a note of almost absurd adulation. Everything their hero does is superhuman, his very faults are turned into virtues. The splendour of the emperor's outward appearance is vividly described. His meanest achievements are compared with the greatest exploits in myth or history, to the detriment of the latter. All the devices of the trained rhetorician are made use of to enhance the speaker's message, the content of which is as much emotional as factual. The language is in general classical and Ciceronian, without any of the archaism of Apuleius or the swollen verbosity of contemporary legal enactments. The speakers had evidently learnt the art of rhetoric from such classicizing manuals as those listed on pp. 73–4. Only Claudius Mamertinus, in his speech to Julian, makes frequent use of poetic words. The speeches are a mine of information for the historian of the period, but of information which must be critically examined; the speakers were not on oath. The collection is also an interesting document of the classicizing culture of the Gaulish upper classes, parallel to that provided for a somewhat later period by Ausonius. Both are marked by a curious unwillingness to look long and seriously at the real world. This very remoteness from everyday circumstances was itself one of the factors which enabled Claudian to replace the prose panegyric by the verse panegyric, which offered greater scope for imagery, adornment and suggestiveness (cf. p. 25).

Quintus Aurelius Symmachus, known also as Eusebius, belonged to one of the most distinguished senatorial families of Rome. His father L. Aurelius Avianius Symmachus, his father-in-law Memmius Vitrasius Orfitus Honorius, and probably his maternal grandfather, had all held the office of Prefect of the City, the normal culmination of a senatorial career at this period. The family owned vast estates in Africa, Numidia, Sicily and southern Italy. Symmachus was born *c.* 345, studied rhetoric at Rome under a teacher from Bordeaux, perhaps Tiberius Victor Minervius who is mentioned in Ausonius' poem on the professors of Bordeaux. We do not know when he held the quaestorship and praetorship, the duties of which were by now limited to giving lavish games. In 365 he was probably *corrector* (governor) of Bruttium, then spent a short time at Valentinian's court in Gaul. In 373–4 he was Proconsul of Africa for eight months. In 384–5 he was Prefect of the City. In 391, as a result of special circumstances, he was appointed one of the consuls of the year, a dignity at this time more often held by generals or court officials than by senators. Twice he took the side of a usurping emperor, first of Maximus in 383 then of Eugenius in 392–4. On both occasions he succeeded in ingratiating himself with Theodosius after the defeat and death of the usurper. His position

as one of the recognized leaders of the senatorial class, whose support Theodosius needed, saved him. He died after 402.

Such was the career of Symmachus. It should be noted that in fact he held
only three offices which involved any serious duties, and each for only about
a year. *Otium* was the way of life of the senatorial class, devoted to managing
their estates – whether energetically or languidly – and pursuing their *dolce
vita* of exquisite good taste, backed by a sure sense of social equalities and
distinctions. Political activity was an interruption of their life, not its main
content. This does not mean that when office interrupted their leisure they did
not take the duties of their posts seriously. As will be seen, Symmachus got
through a great deal of awkward paperwork in his year as Prefect of the City.

He is appreciated today principally for his letters. But during his lifetime he
enjoyed the reputation of being one of the greatest orators of his age. His
erudition was much admired, as was his care for the classics of Roman literature.
There are traces in later manuscripts of recensions of Virgil and Livy prepared
for him. Like many members of the senatorial class, whose spokesman he often
was, Symmachus was a pagan. He combined a Neoplatonizing monotheism
with an antiquarian regard for the traditional religion of the Roman state,
though he could not claim the deep and wide knowledge of sacred lore possessed by his colleague and friend Vettius Agorius Praetextatus. It is one of the
curious ironies of history that it was the pagan Symmachus who recommended
Augustine for the chair of rhetoric in Milan.

Eight speeches by Symmachus survive in a palimpsest manuscript unfortunately in a fragmentary state.[1] They include two panegyric addresses to
Valentinian delivered in 369 and 370, one to his young son and co-emperor
Gratian delivered in 369, two speeches delivered in the senate in 376 and voicing
the relief of the senators at the new political rapprochement between Senate and
emperor, the *Pro Trygetio* and the *Pro patre*, and three further speeches in the
senate on behalf of individuals. We know from his correspondence and elsewhere of many other speeches delivered by Symmachus, and possibly gathered
together in a collected edition, which do not survive. Their style and manner
recall those of the *Panegyrici Latini*. The first three display the forced expressions and occasional lapses of taste characteristic of the panegyric genre.

The letters, though intended by their author for publication, were not in fact
published until after his death, when his son brought out an edition in ten books
comprising some 900 letters written between 364 and 402. Book 10 consists of
the *Relationes*, the official reports sent by Symmachus as Prefect of the City to
the emperor Valentinian II. The model of Pliny's letters evidently prompted
the arrangement of those of Symmachus. The letters are not arranged chronologically, but by addressee, and many of them are impossible to date. They have

[1] Now divided into two parts, cod. Ambrosianus E 147 inf. and cod. Vaticanus latinus 5750.

been described as verbose but empty of content. This is a little harsh. Symmachus well knew that the epistolary genre calls for brevity and compression. And their content was not meant to consist of factual information, but of the affirmation and cultivation of *amicitia*, naturally within a very limited section of late Roman society. The editorial activity of the younger Symmachus may be responsible for some of the bland emptiness of the letters. His father had made many political misjudgements in a long life, which called for excisions and covering of tracks. But the editor cannot have changed the basic tone of the correspondence, which was concerned with social relations and not with information. If information had to be conveyed, it would be conveyed verbally or in a separate enclosure. The letter itself was primarily a work of art. Within the limitations imposed by the rules of the art Symmachus skilfully varies his tone to suit the addressee, striking a philosophical note with Praetextatus, with others affecting archaism, with others a racy informality, with others an irony which sometimes approaches self-parody. But the letters are always studied, never spontaneous. They provide an interesting picture of the intellectual and social interests of a cultivated and idle aristocracy. They contain scarcely any references to the momentous events of the age, in some of which Symmachus was himself involved, though never in a decisive role. The tenth book, the *Relationes*, is a different matter. It contains forty-nine official dispatches sent by Symmachus to the emperor. Some are formal greetings. Many are on complex legal questions involving conflict of laws, which came before the Senate and which were referred to the supreme legislator. Many were in their original state accompanied by dossiers of documents, summaries of evidence and the like, which have not survived. They give an insight into the obsessionally conscientious mode of operation of late Roman government in certain fields. But it must be borne in mind that Symmachus himself was not a bureaucrat. For him office and its responsibilities were fleeting and in some ways regrettable interruptions in a life of *otium* and *amicitia*.

The most striking of the *Relationes* is the plea for the restoration of the altar of Victory in the senate-house. Ever since the days of Augustus senators had offered a pinch of incense on this altar at the outset of the proceedings of the Senate. When Constantius II visited Rome in 357, he had the altar removed, as an offence to Christianity, but it was soon restored to its place, presumably under Julian. In 381 the young emperor Gratian, a devout and even bigoted Christian, the first emperor to drop the title of *Pontifex Maximus*, had the altar removed once more and the revenues of the Vestal Virgins and other Roman priesthoods confiscated. The next year the Senate petitioned for the reversal of these decisions, but Pope Damasus and Ambrose, bishop of Milan, succeeded in persuading Gratian to stick to his decision. After Gratian's death in 383 another petition was organized, and it is this which Symmachus reports

78

to Valentinian II in his famous *Relatio*. It is a balanced and noble plea for religious tolerance, for the avoidance of imposed uniformity, and for respect for the traditions of the past. Naturally, it is the kind of declaration which only threatened minorities make. It did not succeed in its purpose. But it was a sufficiently serious and effective plea to provoke a response from Ambrose (*Epist.* 17) setting out with unequivocal clarity the principle of Christian intolerance. The Christian poet Prudentius also composed a refutation of its arguments (cf. pp. 31–2).

Symmachus was the last great Roman orator in the classical tradition and the last senator whose correspondence was collected and published. But both oratory and epistolography found a new place in the life of the Christian church. The detailed study of this Christian literature falls outside the domain of the present volume. But it may be noted that Ambrose left a collection of 91 letters, Jerome one of 154, and Augustine one of 270. Like the letters of Symmachus, these epistles are works of art, written by men trained in the discipline of literature. But they are unlike those of Symmachus in almost every other respect. They are full of biblical quotation and allusion, which imports a new element into their language. They are often very long. And they are not mere tokens of friendship, but are full of information and argument. The needs of Christian communication broke the narrow bounds within which classical epistolography flourished.

In the same way the Christian sermon was a new form of oratory. We do not possess any sermons of Jerome or Ambrose, at any rate not in their raw form. But an extensive collection of Augustine's *Sermones*, delivered before his congregation at Hippo, survives. The former professor of rhetoric displays a confident command of all the artifices of the discipline. But at the same time he realizes that these artifices may in fact impede communication with an average audience. So he deliberately uses a popular or on occasion vulgar register, quite distinct from that of the *De civitate Dei*: *melius in barbarismo nostro*, he observes, *uos intellegitis quam in nostra disertitudine uos deserti estis* 'It is better for you to understand through my solecism than for you to be left behind by my eloquence' (*Enarr. in psalm.* 36, serm. 3.6); and in another passage he remarks, *melius est reprehendant nos grammatici quam non intellegant populi* 'It is better that grammarians should censure me than that the people should not understand me' (*Enarr. in psalm.* 138.20). It is hard to imagine a more radical break with the tradition of late classical rhetoric.

# 6

## LEARNING AND THE PAST

Macrobius Ambrosius Theodosius, apparently an African, is probably to be identified with the Theodosius who was Praetorian Prefect of Italy in 430. He seems to have been related to the family of the Symmachi. Nothing more is known of his life. But he was evidently an aristocrat rather than a professional scholar. Three works of his survive: the *Commentary on the Dream of Scipio*, the *Saturnalia*, and a treatise *De differentiis et societatibus graeci latinique uerbi*, which is preserved only in excerpts from excerpts made in the Middle Ages. The two former works are dedicated to the writer's son Eustachius.

The *Commentary* is a loose and discursive discussion of the famous dream recounted in Cicero's *De re publica*, in which Scipio Africanus the Elder appears to his grandson, reveals to him his own future destiny and that of his country, expounds the rewards awaiting virtue in the after-life, and describes with impressive majesty the universe and the place of the earth and of man in it. Macrobius does not provide an exhaustive commentary on his text, but launches into a series of expositions in Neoplatonic vein on dreams, on the mystic properties of numbers, on the nature of the soul, on astronomy, on music. He quotes many authorities but it is unlikely that he had read all or even most of them. Plotinus and Porphyry are probably his principal proximate sources, and Virgil is quoted frequently by way of adornment. However the work does embody Neoplatonic thinking which is not directly preserved elsewhere. The style is rather uneven, as Macrobius copies or translates his sources without reducing them to stylistic uniformity.

The *Saturnalia*, in seven books, of which the end of the second and the beginning of the third, the beginning and second half of the fourth, and the ends of the sixth and seventh are missing, purports to be a report at third hand of the discussions of a group of senators and scholars on the three successive days of the Saturnalia in 384. The host on the first day is Vettius Agorius Praetextatus. On the second day the guests assemble in the house of Nicomachus Flavianus, and on the third in that of Q. Aurelius Symmachus. The parallelism in form to some of Cicero's philosophical dialogues – and to such works as Varro's *Res rusticae* – is evident. It may be that Athenaeus' account of an imaginary conversation of scholars at a banquet – the *Deipnosophists* – also contributed to Macrobius' inspiration. The participants in the discussion include, besides the three hosts, the senators Caecina Albinus and Furius Albinus, the grammarian Servius, a young man called Avienus, a Greek rhetorician named Eusebius, a philosopher Eustathius, a doctor Disarius, and an 'uninvited guest' Evangelus. The conversation ranges over a variety of topics, from the terms for various times of day to the history of the *toga praetexta*, from Saturn and Janus to the care shown by the gods for slaves, from jokes to pontifical law. But the central theme, which occupies most of Books 3 to 6, is the poet Virgil. His command of rhetoric, his knowledge of philosophy and astrology, his dependence on Greek sources, his knowledge of Roman religious law and augural practice, his language and metre are all discussed discursively, and interpretations are offered – by Servius – of a number of obscure passages. It is clear that for Macrobius as for Dante Virgil is 'quel Savio gentil, che tutto seppe' (*Inf.* 7.3). The existence of Christianity is completely ignored. The learning displayed by Macrobius is stupendous, if often trifling, and it is backed up by the names of an impressive list of authorities. But Macrobius takes care not to quote the immediate sources from which he gained his information, the principal of which are Aulus Gellius, various commentators on Virgil, and Plutarch's *Quaestiones convivales* in a fuller form than that which we now possess. He did, however, consult other sources from time to time, many of which cannot readily be identified. As in his *Commentary*, so too in his *Saturnalia* he tends to quote his material nearly verbatim. Only the narrative and dramatic framework is really his own.

Macrobius observes that several of the participants were too young to have been present at such a gathering on the dramatic date of December 384 (1.1.5). Recent research has identified the anachronistic participants as Servius and Avienus – who is probably to be identified with the fabulist Avianus or Avienus (p. 36). These and other considerations – such as the posthumous rehabilitation of Nicomachus Flavianus in 430 from the disgrace of espousing the cause of the usurper Eugenius – have led recently to the suggestion of a new date for the composition of the *Saturnalia*, which used to be dated at the beginning of the fifth century. It now seems likely to have been written shortly after 430. This means that it is not a picture of cultivated pagan senatorial society by a man who knew it from personal observation. It is rather a sentimental re-evocation of a lost world which was rapidly becoming idealized. In the harsh environment of 430, when Rome had been sacked by Alaric, when barbarian invasions were tearing whole provinces out of the fabric of the empire, there were still men who liked to look back on the civilized elegance of life in *la belle époque.* That they probably did not understand all its nuances did not diminish their nostalgia, but it no doubt resulted in a certain rigidity and formalism in its depiction. The picture painted by Macrobius of late fourth-century senatorial society is the very antithesis of that provided by Ammianus Marcellinus. But it is probably going too far to suggest that the desire to rebut Ammianus was high among Macrobius' motives. Wooden and mechanical as much of it is, the *Saturnalia* is a touching picture of the nostalgia of a class which had been overtaken by events, not the least among which was the conversion to Christianity of the great bulk of the Roman aristocracy. But there is no controversial intent behind the dialogue; classical culture and pagan religion are simply assumed without question to be identical.

About the same time as Macrobius was completing his *Saturnalia* in Rome, Martianus Capella published in Carthage his *Marriage of Mercury and Philology*, one of the most extraordinary works in all Latin literature, and in some ways more indicative of the spirit of the age than the sober and dignified exchanges of Macrobius' bookish grandees. Of Martianus Min(n)e(i)us Felix Capella little is known save that he lived in Carthage and wrote his book in his old age. He may have been a teacher of rhetoric. The short autobiographical poem which concludes his work has been transmitted in so corrupt a form as to be virtually useless; but one passage in it may indicate that he practised as an advocate in the proconsular court at Carthage. The date of the work is equally unclear; probably after 410, because of an allusion to the sack of Rome, certainly before 439, when Carthage passed into the hands of the Vandals. Earlier dates have been proposed, but the arguments in their favour carry little conviction.

The *De Nuptiis Mercurii et Philologiae*, in nine books, is an encyclopaedia of the liberal arts set in an allegorical narrative framework. Short poems are interspersed through the prose text in the manner of the *Satura Menippea*. The first two books describe, with a wealth of elaborate fancy, the selection of a bride for Mercury (the god of eloquence) in the person of Philology, her preparation and purification for the marriage, her ascent to the astral heaven, the diverse guests, human and divine, there assembled, and finally the marriage ceremony itself. Philology is accompanied in her ascent to the higher world by seven *feminae dotales* – not bridesmaids, but slave women forming part of the bride's dowry – each representing one of the seven liberal arts. In Books 3 to 9 they give each in turn a systematic account of the art which they represent, in the order Grammar, Dialectic, Rhetoric, Geometry, Arithmetic, Astronomy and Music. The account of the marriage in Books 1 and 2 is certainly inspired by the marriage of Cupid and Psyche in Apuleius' *Metamorphoses*. But there is much more to it than that. The description of the stages through which Philology passes on the way to her apotheosis reflects the actual liturgy of the Neoplatonist mystic worship of Hecate, into which Julian had been initiated by Maximus of Ephesus, with its syncretism of Orphic, Neopythagorean and Chaldean elements. Whether Martianus owed his acquaintance with this liturgy to a literary tradition now lost or to a ritual tradition of clandestine paganism is an open question. A third element pervading the whole of Books 1 and 2 is the elaborate allegorical interpretation given of all the events recounted. If Prudentius was the father of Christian allegory, Martianus is at the origin of profane allegory in the European tradition.

The succeeding books vary in scope and systematic treatment. Grammar (Book 3) starts with exhaustive discussion of letters and syllables, goes on to the parts of speech, declension and conjugation, then to a long discussion of analogy and finally a short section on anomaly. The proximate sources cannot be identified. But Martianus' doctrine does not differ significantly from that of other grammarians of the fourth and fifth centuries. Dialectic (Book 4) is an account of Aristotelian formal logic interspersed in a rather muddled way with precepts on practical rhetoric, and with some remarkable omissions. The sources probably include Varro – whether directly or indirectly – Porphyry's *Isagoge* and Aristotle's *Categories* via a Latin adaptation, and Apuleius' Περὶ ἑρμηνείας. The section on Rhetoric (Book 5) uses Cicero's *De inventione* as a prime source but also draws on Cicero's other rhetorical works and the commentaries on them by Marius Victorinus, as well as on the manuals of rhetoric of the late Empire. Martianus seems indeed to have used a greater variety of sources here than in any other section, which lends support to the conjecture that he was a teacher of rhetoric. The section on Geometry (Book 6) does not consist, like the preceding sections, of definitions, axioms and propositions, but is mainly made up by a geographical survey of the known world in the form of long lists of place-names with occasional comments. Only at the end of this does the allegorical lady admit that she has been digressing, and gives a very brief and inadequate introduction to Euclidean geometry, with the excuse that the lateness of the hour precludes a systematic treatment. The main source is Solinus' *Collectanea rerum memorabilium* and Pliny's geographical books (3–6). Martianus either could not handle Euclidean geometry – he makes a complete hash of Eratosthenes' method of measuring the circumference of the earth – or believed that his readers would not understand it. And indeed it would be difficult to provide a satisfactory exposition without the use of diagrams. For this reason he filled out the space allocated to geometry with this curious geographical farrago. The section on Arithmetic (Book 7) – by which is meant not computation but the theory of numbers – is mainly a digest of the *Introduction to arithmetic* of Nicomachus of Gerasa and of Books 7 to 9 of Euclid's *Elements*. Martianus is unlikely to have used either in the original, and one can only speculate on his proximate sources. The whole exposition is overlaid by a stratum of numerology and mysticism not to be found in Nicomachus or Euclid. This section is one of the most systematically arranged in the whole work. Astronomy makes her entry in a kind of space-ship before expounding her art. Her discourse (Book 8) is perhaps the best exposition of classical geocentric astronomy available in Latin until the twelfth century and enjoyed immense influence. It may stem originally from a handbook by Varro derived from Posidonius, but we can only guess at Martianus' immediate source. Finally Harmony or Music (Book 9) enters, and after reciting a long list of instances of the emotional or therapeutic effects of music gives a digest of classical musical and metrical theory drawn entirely from Aristides Quintilianus' Περὶ μουσικῆς 'On music' (1.1–19). At the conclusion of her discourse the gods lead the bride and bridegroom to the marriage chamber. There follows an autobiographical poem of 27 lines, so flamboyant in expression and so corruptly transmitted as to be practically unintelligible.

Martianus writes a baroque and convoluted Latin often of extreme obscurity. His vocabulary comprises many neologisms, either new compounds or derivatives such as *hiatimembris, astriloquus, dulcineruis, uernicomus, latrocinaliter, perendinatio, interriuatio,* or technical words, often of Greek origin, such as *acronychus, egersimon, helicoeides.* When he is setting out stock handbook material, his style is fairly prosaic, though usually long-winded. But in his narrative and above all in his descriptive passages, and thus particularly in Books 1 and 2, he uses a florid style, overloaded with abstract nouns, with imagery and word-play, which has no parallel in classical Latin. His desire for self-expression evidently exceeded his capacity, and the result is often a torrent of words which obscure rather than reveal his meaning. In his verse passages the language, style and metre are more classical, so far as the often defective transmission enables us to judge. There was evidently a strong strain of exhibitionism about Martianus, visual as well as verbal. His descriptions, particularly of the remarkable allegorical ladies, are vivid in detail and not without lasciviousness. These features of content and language, together with the allegorical narrative framework, ensured his book conspicuous success from the Carolingian age to the Renaissance, in spite of the mediocrity of the information which it contained. What we should like to know, but cannot, is what kind of reader Martianus had in mind in his own day. He is too difficult for schoolboys and too inadequate for scholars.

## 2. GRAMMARIANS

Throughout the period under review grammar, in its Hellenistic sense of the systematic study of language and literature, continued to form the main content of the education of those who proceeded beyond mere practical ability to read and write. In every city of the Latin-speaking world *grammatici* – sometimes holding public appointments – drilled their pupils in letters, syllables and words, instilled the doctrine of the parts of speech, their distinctions and inflections, taught the principles of metre, and illustrated their precepts by reading and commenting on classical Latin poets, above all Terence and Virgil. Prose writers were mainly left to the teachers of rhetoric.

Of the many text-books and manuals written – and in a sense each teacher produced his own text-book – only a few survive, and they have few original features. The pattern of the *Ars grammatica* had been set long ago by such men as Remmius Palaemon, who in their turn built upon the work of their Greek predecessors. The grammarians of late antiquity drew on their classical forerunners through the grammarians and scholars of the Antonine and Severan age. A brief survey will therefore suffice. Towards the end of the third century, probably in the reign of Diocletian, Marius Plotius Sacerdos wrote his *Artes grammaticae* in three books, the third of which treated metre. He still quotes many Greek examples in the course of explaining Latin grammar and metre. From the early part of the second half of the fourth century we have three surviving manuals of grammar. The *Ars grammatica* in five books of Flavius Sosipater Charisius, probably to be identified with an African appointed to a public chair of grammar in Constantinople in 358, deals with the traditional topics of grammar in the first three books, and with metre and stylistics in the last two. The fifth book is incomplete. Charisius' grammar is a rather mechanical compilation from earlier works. About the same time Diomedes published his *Ars grammatica* in three books. In the first he deals with the parts of speech, goes on to treat the elementary principles of grammar and to discuss questions of style in the second, and expounds the principles of metre in the third. This unusual order of treatment is probably determined by practical considerations of teaching, and offers an interesting example of the ability of these tradition-bound scholars to innovate. The relation between Diomedes and Charisius cannot be determined with certainty. They draw on too many common sources.

Aelius Donatus, Jerome's teacher, is recorded as flourishing in 353. His *Ars grammatica* in two versions, elementary and advanced (*Ars minor* and *Ars maior*) is a shorter work than those of Charisius and Diomedes, with whom he shared common sources. In clarity of exposition and judicious selection of material it far surpasses them. The longer work covers in more detail the same ground as the shorter, but omits the more elementary topics such as verb paradigms. It was evidently meant to be studied after the *Ars minor*. Donatus was clearly an unusually gifted teacher. Jerome enjoyed every minute of his schooldays, and remembered his old master with warmth in his old age in distant Bethlehem. Donatus' grammar soon became a standard work, in so far as such a thing existed before the invention of printing. A dense thicket of commentaries grew up around it, the earliest surviving those by Servius in the early fifth century and by Cledonius and Pompeius a little later, further commentaries being composed by Julian of Toledo in the late seventh century and Remigius of Auxerre about 900. Donatus' Latin grammar became a classic just as had the Greek grammar of Dionysius the Thracian, and each dominated the study of its respective language in the Middle Ages. Donatus also wrote commentaries on Virgil and Terence. That on Virgil is lost but for the introduction. That on Terence survives, though probably in somewhat modified form. It is a work of notable scholarship, dealing not only with language but also with problems of staging and the relation of Terence to his Greek models. What it does not provide, and from its form as a line by line commentary cannot, is adequate discussion of structure, dramatic form and character.

Jerome's teacher of rhetoric, C. Marius Victorinus Afer, was a man of immense learning and deep philosophical interests. Indeed he was the intellectual leader of the Roman Neoplatonists in the middle of the fourth century. His works include an *Ars grammatica* in four books which deals almost exclusively with metre. It was meant for advanced students. But his main influence was exercised through his series of translations of Greek philosophical works, from Plato through Aristotle to Plotinus and Porphyry. He also wrote commentaries on Aristotle's logical works and on Cicero's *De inventione*. His conversion to Christianity in his old age was a scandal to his pagan admirers and followers. As a Christian he wrote polemical anti-Arian treatises, a commentary on the Pauline epistles, a poem, with many Virgilian echoes, on the Maccabaean brothers, and possibly hymns in hexameters. Victorinus provides an interesting example of the adaptation of the traditional skills of the pagan scholar to new Christian ends. His works survive only in part.

Among the interlocutors in Macrobius' *Saturnalia* there is a young man named Servius, who elucidates Virgil. It has been convincingly argued that his presence at such a gathering in 384 is an anachronism, and that his active literary activity falls within the fifth century. His long commentary on Virgil probably belongs to the 20s of that century. It illumines for us as no other work can the way in which men of culture in late antiquity studied the masterpieces of their literary heritage. Servius' careful and sometimes almost reverent observations cover the whole range of Virgilian scholarship, from elementary points of language to Virgil's creative use of his Greek and Latin models. His commentary is particularly rich in antiquarian information – not all of equal reliability – on early Italy. The presentation is not dogmatic; often he sets out two interpretations and leaves the choice to the reader. His material is largely drawn from the older commentators on Virgil – Probus, Asper, and others – but Servius is no mere mechanical compiler. His own judgement, often expressed, is sound rather than original. A devoted and gifted pedagogue as well as a scholar, he succeeds in conveying much of the richness of classical Roman study of Virgil, firmly based on the text and eschewing the flights of allegorizing imagination of many later interpreters. His shortcomings are those of any literary critic who restricts himself, in the classical manner, to line by line and word by word explication. Yet without Servius, our understanding of Virgil today would be both narrower and shallower. The text survives in two recensions. In the longer of these – the so-called Servius Danielis – Servius' original commentary has been supplemented, probably in the seventh or eighth century, by material from other commentators, including Aelius Donatus. Much of this supplementary material is of the utmost value. A good critical text of the whole of Servius is still lacking. Servius also wrote a commentary on the two versions of the *Ars grammatica* of Donatus and several minor grammatical and metrical treatises.

Finally, there survives under the name of Claudius Donatus a rhetorical and stylistic commentary on Virgil. This mediocre work, which takes for granted the linguistic and material explication which forms the bulk of Servius' commentary, reminds us that Virgil was studied not only by grammarians but also by rhetoricians, who sought in his works illustrations of the concepts of their science. This interest of the rhetorician in Virgil is part of a larger phenomenon characteristic of late antiquity, the blurring of the boundaries between prose and poetry and the loss of feeling for the appropriateness of literary genres.

A rather different kind of grammatical activity is represented by the *De compendiosa doctrina* of Nonius Marcellus, an African who was probably active in the first half of the fourth century. His vast compilation is a lexicon of Republican Latin. The first twelve books are arranged grammatically, i.e. the entries are based on words or forms, the remaining eight are organized by subject matter, e.g. articles of clothing, weapons. The entries in each case are substantially of the same character, and consist of brief definitions supported by a series of citations from Republican authors. Nonius Marcellus was evidently reaching across the gap of the third century to the antiquarian scholarship of the age of Fronto, Aulus Gellius and Apuleius. His lexicon with its copious quotations is the product of the habit of making excerpts which Fronto tried to instil into his students. Nonius Marcellus works largely at second hand, from earlier collections of excerpts rather than from the original texts. His ignorance and inattention diminish but cannot destroy the value of his compilation. Without him our knowledge of such major Republican writers as Lucilius, Pacuvius and Accius would be sadly reduced.

# 7

## MINOR FIGURES

Astrology was believed in and practised by all classes in the Late Empire. The Neoplatonist doctrine of a hierarchical universe provided an intellectual foundation for astrology which made it acceptable as a science and conferred on its practitioners new respectability and dignity. Only the Christians condemned astrology out of hand. And the frequency with which the Church Fathers repeat their denunciations of the art suggests that it had many adherents even in Christian communities. Shortly before the middle of the fourth century Julius Firmicus Maternus, a Sicilian of senatorial rank who had practised as an advocate, completed his handbook of astrology – *Matheseos libri VIII*. It is dedicated to Q. Flavius Maesius Egnatius Lollianus, otherwise Mavortius, *comes Orientis* 330–6, proconsul of Africa 334–7, Prefect of the City of Rome 342, consul 355, Praetorian Prefect 355–6, who had encouraged Maternus to write his manual.[1]

In his first book Maternus defends astrology against sceptical criticism and alleges that he was the first to introduce the science to Rome. By this he means that he was the first to write a treatise on the subject in Latin. His claim is in fact unfounded, as Manilius had written on the subject in verse three centuries earlier. But Maternus may not have known of Manilius' poem, and the many resemblances between the two are likely to be due to the use of common sources in Greek. The remaining seven books set out in great detail, with many examples, the principles of the alleged science. Maternus' treatise is the longest and most systematic exposition of astrology surviving from antiquity. He has a lofty concept of his calling and demands of the astrologer the highest moral standards and the most circumspect behaviour, including refraining from attending the Circus lest he be thought to influence the results of the races. Maternus never squarely faces the inconsistency between the strict determinism which he postulates in human affairs – only the emperor is exempt – and the moral responsibility of the individual.

His style is uneven. Much of his treatise is in the simple, no-nonsense style appropriate to scientific writing. But from time to time he launches into elabo-

[1] On Mavortius' possible family connexions cf. Arnheim (1972) 136–7.

rate rhetorical purple passages. In these he tends to run his metaphors on to the point of absurdity. His vocabulary includes many late Latin words such as *concordialis, mansuetarius, quiescentia*, and he is particularly fond of *intimare*. He mentions a number of other astrological works which he has written, but these do not survive.

There also exists a work of Christian anti-pagan polemic, *De errore profanarum religionum* 'On the error of profane religions', attributed to Julius Firmicus Maternus *vir clarissimus* and written, on internal evidence, about the middle of the fourth century. It is a savage attack on pagan cults and mysteries, which it sees as the work of the devil. It provides valuable information on pagan religious practices in late antiquity. It has generally been believed that its author is the Firmicus Maternus who wrote on astrology, and that the second work is the fruit of his conversion to Christianity. But the matter cannot be proved, and the two writers could well be brothers or cousins or totally unrelated. There is certainly a difference of tone between the two works. The astrologer is solemn and composed, the Christian fiery and combative. But the zeal of the convert may be the explanation. No significant differences in linguistic usage have been noted. If both works are by the same author they provide an interesting document in the intellectual history of the fourth century.

Some time in the late fourth or early fifth century Palladius Rutilius Taurus Aemilianus, *vir illustris*, wrote a handbook of agriculture, the precise title of which is uncertain. After an introductory book dealing with agriculture in general, Books 2 to 13 set out the tasks of the farmer month by month. Book 14, which was not discovered until the present century, deals with the care of farm animals and the rudiments of veterinary science. The work is completed by a poem in 85 elegiac couplets on the grafting of fruit-trees. Palladius evidently models his book on that of Columella, whom he frequently draws on, sometimes copying him almost word for word. But the tone and style of the work are quite different from those of Columella. The rhetorical veneer of Columella is absent, and Palladius writes very simple, clear Latin, without any attempt at producing a work of *belles lettres*. And the scientific treatment of agriculture, which Columella inherited from his Greek forbears, is abandoned in favour of a series of short recipes or instructions for dealing with particular practical problems.

Palladius' main source is Gargilius Martialis (first half of the third century), of whose handbook of agriculture only a few fragments survive. But he also makes extensive use of Columella – particularly Books 2, 6–9, and 11, of the epitome of Vitruvius by Faventinus, and occasionally of the lost Greek Συναγωγή γεωργικῶν ἐπιτηδευμάτων of Anatolius of Beirut (written *c.* 361). He occasionally adds observations based on his own experience as a landowner. Some of these throw a revealing light on the agrarian world of late antiquity, e.g. the remark that a broken column was handy for levelling a threshing-floor (7.1). The strictly practical orientation of Palladius' handbook made it a favourite in the Middle Ages. A Middle English translation exists. There were also translations into Italian and Catalan in the fourteenth century.

Flavius Vegetius Renatus, who held the rank of *comes*, published his *Epitoma rei militaris* 'All the soldier needs to know' in four books after 383 and before 450. The emperor to whom it is dedicated is probably Theodosius I, but could be Valentinian III or even Theodosius II. The author is a Christian, but not a *dévot*. Book 1 deals with the selection and training of recruits, Book 2 with military organization, Book 3 with tactics and strategy, Book 4 with engines of war and – briefly – with naval warfare. There is much lamentation about the decline of the Roman army and the need to return to ancient models and practices. There is a curious patina of antiquity over the whole work, even when the author is writing about the army of his own day. In fact he draws much of his information from earlier sources, such as Cato, Celsus and Frontinus, and fails to distinguish clearly between what happened in the past – and ought to happen now – and the military realities of the present. Each book is preceded by a rhetorical preface and followed by a rhetorical conclusion. The bulk of the work is written in a plain, businesslike style, appropriate for technical writing, and open to neologisms. The same Vegetius is almost certainly the author of a veterinary handbook – *Mulomedicina* – based largely on Celsus, Pelagonius and on the so-called *Mulomedicina Chironis*, a manual of veterinary medicine written in rather unclassical Latin. Indeed much of Vegetius is a rewriting at a somewhat higher stylistic level of the *Mulomedicina Chironis*.

Another work, this time anonymous, also deals with the military problems of the Late Empire. Entitled *De rebus bellicis*, the little treatise of about fifteen printed pages was written between 337 and 378, and probably in the period 366 to 375. It puts forward proposals for the reduction of public expenditure, spread of tax liability, reform of the mint, and introduction of a number of new articles of military equipment. These include a kind of armoured chariot with movable scythe blades, a felt undershirt to wear beneath armour, a portable bridge supported by bladders, a warship driven by paddles worked by oxen, a super-ballista and the like. It is hard to say whether the author is a serious military reformer or a member of the lunatic fringe. His work is probably a fortuitous survivor from many proposals for reform in the Late Empire duly submitted, docketed and forgotten. Few reformers, however, can have had such a touching faith in gadgetry.

Arnobius, a pagan teacher of rhetoric and advocate from Sicca Veneria (Le Kef) in Africa, born *c*. 240, was impressed by the bearing of Christians haled before the courts during Diocletian's persecution (302–4). Eventually he experienced a sudden conversion to Christianity. The local bishop was at first suspicious of his good faith, and asked for evidence of the sincerity of his conversion. Arnobius thereupon wrote his apologetic treatise *Adversus nationes* 'Against the Gentiles' and was as a result accepted into the Christian community. The treatise is in seven books. The first two defend the Christian religion against the popular charge that it is responsible for the present misfortunes of the Roman world, as well as against more philosophical objections. The remaining five are devoted to an onslaught on the paganism of his time; Books 3 and 4 deal with pagan mythology, Books 5 to 7 with cult practices.

Arnobius knew little about Christianity when he composed his work; he does not understand the divinity of Christ, supposes human souls to be by their nature mortal and to acquire immortality through merit, and shows little acquaintance with the Christian scriptures. On the other hand he knew a great deal about the theory and practice of pagan belief and ritual. His book is a mine of information on myths and cults and in general on the religious concepts and practices of the educated but unphilosophical Roman citizen of his time. Though he shows scarcely any signs of Neoplatonist influence, he was familiar with the vaguely philosophical syncretism of much late Roman religion.

His method is to score debating points. Wit, ridicule and the discovery of apparent contradictions are his instruments. As befits a professional rhetorician he handles them with aplomb. Apostrophe, exclamation, rhetorical question, syllogism, and enthymeme follow one another with dizzy rapidity. All the contradictions of his opponent's position are revealed with merciless thoroughness but little real profundity. Antithesis, alliteration, homoeoteleuton and other figures of speech abound. Arnobius uses a wide-ranging vocabulary, including many archaisms and poetic words, and often piles synonym upon synonym for the same idea. As a display of rhetorical pyrotechnics his treatise has few rivals. As a serious contribution to its declared subject its value is negligible. It is noteworthy that his style is very different from the sober, rather dull Ciceronianism of the contemporary Gaulish orators whose speeches survive in the *Panegyrici Latini*. Perhaps the influence of Apuleius and Tertullian was still strong in their native land.

# 8

# APULEIUS

Apuleius (no *praenomen* is attested) was born at Madauros (Mdaurusch in Algeria) in the middle 120s A.D., the son of a wealthy duumvir. His *Apology* sketches the main lines of his earlier career. Having studied locally at Carthage under the *grammaticus* and *rhetor* and having developed philosophical interests there, he continued his researches for some years at Athens and spent a period in Rome. By the time of his chance arrival at Oea (Tripoli) in 155–6, he was a literary celebrity. His marriage there to Pudentilla, a wealthy widow, led to indictment on a charge of magic. After acquittal he resided in Carthage, his life as sophist and leading dignitary being documented in his *Florida*. Nothing is known of any activities after about A.D. 170.

In the history of Latin literature Apuleius has two main claims to attention. As a philosopher without original genius he is important for his transmission of the ideas of Middle Platonism, and as a writer of fiction he is the author of the *Metamorphoses* ('Transformations'), the one Latin romance to have survived complete from the classical period. These contributions have traditionally been studied in isolation from each other, to the impoverishment of criticism of the *Metamorphoses*. The student of the novel cannot adequately assess its nature and purpose without prior investigation of its author's leading attitudes and preoccupations.

Everything that the man touches reflects the curiosity of the scientist or the enthusiasm of the philosophical littérateur. Practical treatises on trees, agriculture, medicines; a long compilation in Greek on natural history (*Quaestiones naturales*); educational works on astronomy, music, arithmetic, as well as a disquisition on proverbs; light verses after the manner of Catullus of both a risqué and a satirical kind; symposium-literature in the manner of Gellius or Athenaeus; in the sphere of fiction, in addition to the *Metamorphoses* a second romance *Hermagoras*, an anthology of love-anecdotes, not to mention a mysterious *Epitome historiarum* – no one seriously regrets the loss of much of this, but the catalogue indicates the author's phenomenal intellectual energy. Yet his main concerns lay beyond these enthusiasms. Philosophy was his major love; in addition to his surviving volumes he composed a *De re publica*,

('On the commonwealth') and a translation of Plato's *Phaedo*. He had also a reputation as a public speaker, and the *Apology* and *Florida* allow us to gauge his effectiveness as advocate and sophist.

I

The *Apologia* (more correctly *Apulei Platonici pro se de magia*) was a speech of self-defence delivered before the proconsul Claudius Maximus at Sabrata in 158–9. After his marriage to Pudentilla, widowed mother of his undergraduate friend Pontianus, an envious indictment on a charge of magic had been laid by Sicinius Aemilius, brother of Pudentilla's first husband, on behalf of Pontianus' brother Sicinius Pudens. An additional charge of the murder of Pontianus was hastily dropped. Conviction for magic under the *lex Cornelia de sicariis et veneficiis* of Sulla could have been punishable by death, but Apuleius' characteristically witty, learned, long-winded oration demolished the flimsy fabric of charges like a sledgehammer cracking a nut.

Within the conventional frame of exordium and peroration, Apuleius structures the content idiosyncratically but firmly under three separate issues. In the first section he rebuts attacks on the manner of his private life with the techniques of the public lecturer, regaling the court-president with disquisitions on 'The private innocence of the lascivious versifier', 'The proper deployment of the mirror', 'The enlightened master', 'The true nature of poverty', and interlarding these with a host of quotations from Greek and Latin poetry. Having comfortably established his cultural and moral superiority over his opponents, he proceeds to his second section, in which he demonstrates that the 'magical malpractices' were the zoological studies befitting a second Aristotle, the medical researches of an aspiring Hippocrates, and the religious devotions befitting a Roman Platonist. (The distinction drawn here between the devotee of magic and the true philosopher should be weighed by students of the *Metamorphoses*.) The third section crisply delineates events at Oea since the defendant's arrival, and in shattering the arguments of the prosecution Apuleius attains an urgency of argumentation worthy of Cicero himself.

The gulf which divides this proficient litigant from the forensic achievements of a Republican advocate is manifest in the more professorial style of address, in the occasionally outlandish diction, in the sudden bursts of luxuriant antithesis. But the effective technique in the later speech indicates how much Apuleius has learnt from the best orators. Cicero would have been proud to own him as a disciple.

The *Florida* (lit. 'Flowery things'), a collection of twenty-three extracts from published speeches and lectures, contains little of intrinsic interest but offers useful documentation on the activities and status of Apuleius after his return to Carthage. The few evidences of dating are confined to the 160s, and the snatches of civic addresses to Roman officials, references to tenure of the chief priesthood and to honorific statues, and the pungent odour of complacent self-satisfaction reveal him as the province's social lion of that decade. The passages have a homogeneity in that each is part of a personal exordium prefacing a speech or lecture, the content being polite philosophy for everyman. Apuleius makes his public appearances as the African Plutarch, discoursing now on the life-style of Hippias or Crates, now on the voyages of Pythagoras or the gymnosophists of India.

## II

The extant philosophical works traditionally attributed to Apuleius are *De deo Socratis*, *De Platone et eius dogmate*, *De mundo*, Περὶ ἑρμηνείας, and *Asclepius*. The authenticity of the first is generally accepted, though the *praefatio* is now assigned to the *Florida*. Scholars have been divided about the second and third because of their less exuberant style, but this may be explicable not only by an earlier date but also by the likelihood that the *De deo Socratis* was *declaimed* whereas the other two were written with no epideictic intent for a reading public. The content and attitudes revealed in the works encourage attribution of them to Apuleius, as does identification of the author by the manuscripts and by Augustine. The Περὶ ἑρμηνείας ('On interpretation') has less well authenticated claims, for it appears in a separate manuscript-tradition, and is more jejune in content; it cannot however be dismissed out of hand as non-Apuleian. The *Asclepius* is a Latin translation by an unknown hand of a lost Greek hermetic work. This brief survey of Apuleius' importance as philosopher concentrates on the first three of the five treatises.

*De deo Socratis* ('On Socrates' god') is a thoroughly misleading title, for Apuleius' primary concern is to preach the existence of demons in general; the treatise has immense importance in the history of ideas as the most systematic exposition of the subject from the ancient world. With admirable clarity of structure the first section surveys the separated worlds of gods (visible stars and invisible members of the Pantheon) and of men; the second part describes the place of demons in the hierarchy of rational beings as intermediaries between the two. After outlining their role and nature, Apuleius assigns them into three classes. The first are souls within human bodies. The second have quitted human shape to become Lemures, Lares, Larvae, Manes. The third are wholly free of bodily connexions, being endowed with special powers and allotted specific duties. Somnus and Amor are offered as examples, the second being of particular interest to the student of the *Metamorphoses*. The nature of Socrates' demon forms the final section; Apuleius labels it *deus* because this is the word familiar to his readers from Cicero and Ovid. The protreptic conclusion exhorting those readers to embrace wisdom incorporates numerous motifs of the Roman diatribe from Horace and Seneca.

Though the treatise reflects familiarity with Plato, the subject of the hierarchy of intelligent creatures and their demarcated regions owes more to Plato's successors from Xenocrates onwards. The work is a contribution to a lively debate within Middle Platonism, perhaps a counterblast to the more rationalistic approach of an Albinus; for Apuleius is heir to Plutarch in his exploitation of the Platonist philosophy to justify popular piety and confidence in the beneficence of a transcendent god. The texture of the work, with its evocation of Latin poetry (Lucretius and Virgil are pervasive) and baroque Latinity, categorizes it as the *conférence brillante* of the literary salon. The author's fervid evangelism is overlaid with the bland veneer of the man of letters.

By contrast *De Platone et eius dogmate* ('On Plato and his doctrines') is written in the more restrained style appropriate to a summary of philosophical teaching composed for a reading public. The work is an outline in two books of Plato's physics and ethics. Such a synthesis if original would have been an impressive achievement. But the similar organization of topics in Albinus' teaching-manual of Plato's doctrines may indicate that both are reproducing with different emphases the schematic annotations of an earlier philosopher of the Middle Porch. Albinus, more professional, prefaces his discussion of Plato's physics and ethics with a section on logic; though Apuleius promises such a threefold analysis, Plato's logic is never treated. (It may have appeared in the lacuna at the end of Book 1, but more probably Apuleius found the subject too dry and abstruse. The gap between promise and performance has encouraged commentators from Cassiodorus onwards to regard Περὶ ἑρμηνείας as Apuleian.)

The discussion of Plato's physics is preceded by a hagiographical life, important as preceding the not dissimilar account of Diogenes Laertius. The treatment of physics is faithful to the *Timaeus* and *Republic*, but the explanation of ethical tenets owes more to the post-Platonist tradition. Middle Platonism, beginning with the eclectic Antiochus of Ascalon, had incorporated Peripatetic and Stoic elements into its developed system, and this later systematization Apuleius misleadingly attributes to Plato himself. The brief appendix on politics draws more faithfully on *Republic* and *Laws*. The importance of this treatise is twofold; it offers precious evidence of the intellectual history of Middle Platonism, and its bold simplifications provide leading indications of the author's intellectual and religious preoccupations, not to be ignored in analysis of the *Metamorphoses*.

*De mundo* ('On the world') likewise addressed to Faustinus, is a close adaptation (unacknowledged) of ps.-Aristotle's Περὶ κόσμου, which was composed about the time of the birth of Christ. The treatise is divided into two sections. The longer part is devoted to cosmology, beginning with an account of the aether and descending thereafter to various aspects of earth. After a bridging discussion on the harmony between constituent parts of the earth, the second section is devoted to theology; God, known to men under different names (compare the Isiac aretalogy in the final book of the *Metamorphoses*), animates and preserves all things. Systematic comparison with the original reveals how Apuleius has lent his translation a Roman flavour for his Roman audience. There is citation of Roman as well as Greek poetry. Various concordant aspects of city-life at Rome are adduced to exemplify the harmony in the larger world. Beyond these cultural changes, minor divergences reveal the translator's philosophical predilections. He stresses the higher significance of the theological facet, claiming that God can be known only through meditation. There is more emphasis than in the original on the concord in the world, and less on its eternity. The distinction in the Greek between God's transcendent *ousia* and his immanent *dunamis* is adapted to accommodate the demons of *De deo Socratis*. Style and latinity occupy a position intermediate between that of *De deo Socratis* and that of *De Platone*; occasional evocations and rhythmical riots reveal the characteristics of the first, but the general presentation is more akin to the sobriety of the second, perhaps lending substance to the notion that *De mundo* and *De Platone* were composed at Rome in the 150s.

## III

It is right to treat Apuleius' novel as the climax of his work not because a late date is indisputable (though the probabilities support composition in Africa after 160) but because it is the most original and the most justifiably celebrated of his writings. Augustine remarks that Apuleius called it *Asinus aureus*, 'The golden ass', but the manuscript-evidence favours the title *Metamorphoses*. The plural would appear inapposite if the hero-narrator Lucius did not make it clear in the proem that the theme is transformation and restoration of 'men's shapes and fortunes'. So the title embraces not only Lucius' changes of shape but also his changes of fortune, above all his spiritual conversion; and it makes ancillary reference to the changes wrought in other characters like Thelyphron, experiencing a change of countenance, and Psyche, who achieves apotheosis.

In spite of its unusual aggregate of eleven books, the romance is carefully structured. In 1–3 Lucius describes how he visited Thessalian Hypata, embroiled himself in a casual affair with a slave-girl, persuaded her to assist his metamorphosis into a bird, and was accidentally changed into an ass; this initial section includes also Aristomenes' account of how his friend Socrates lost his life at the hands of a witch, Thelyphron's testimony of how his rash offer to guard a corpse led to his facial mutilation, and the episode of Lucius' 'trial' at the Festival of Laughter. The second section (4–7.14) describes how robbers drive the human donkey off to their mountain-lair, and how after an abortive attempt at escape with the kidnapped maiden Charite he is freed with her by her lover Tlepolemus; the lawless society of the brigands is depicted in three anecdotes, but the central feature is the tale of Psyche extending over two books, told to Charite by an old woman who tends the robbers. The third section (7.15–10) strings together the grisly, cruel and comic experiences of the ass as he works successively on a farm, with mendicant priests, in a bakery, in a market garden, and in the retinue of a landowner Thiasus; these experiences, prefaced with the pathetic tale of Charite's death, are interspersed with patterned episodes of conjugal infidelity and destructive magic. In the fourth and climactic section Lucius escapes the prospect of public copulation with a female criminal at Corinth by bolting to the nearby shore at Cenchreae. His prayer for deliverance is answered by Isis' promise that the morrow will bring deliverance. A priest in an Isiac procession duly proffers him roses; in gratitude for his restoration to human shape, Lucius becomes successively an initiate of Isis at Corinth and of Osiris at Rome.

Lucius in the prologue calls this a story adapted from the Greek (*fabula Graecanica*). The original Greek story, whose author the ninth-century patriarch Photius calls 'Lucius of Patrae', is now lost, but an abridged version of it appears in the works of Lucian, the most probable candidate for the authorship of the original. This short story, the *Onos* ('Ass'), reveals that Apuleius has followed the original narrative closely, but with two important enlargements. First, he has transformed the climax. In the Greek version the ass was taken not to Corinth but to Thessalonika, and he escaped public copulation with the female criminal by devouring rose-petals carried by a visitor in the amphitheatre; after restoration to human shape he eventually sailed home. So the entirely different climax in the Latin novel has been grafted on by Apuleius himself. Secondly, various anecdotes and episodes have been sewn into the original to fulfil Lucius' initial promise, *uarias fabulas conseram* 'I shall string together sundry tales'.

The extent to which Apuleius is responsible for this anecdotal material is controverted. Scholars' opinions range from the 'minimalist' position, in which little more than *Cupid and Psyche* and the more sentimental stories are conceded to him, to the more popular thesis, assumed in this discussion, that our novelist has transformed a Greek short story into a full-length romance by incorporation of all the episodes not contained in the *Onos*. It is relevant to remember here both that Apuleius was a professional collector of stories and that the works of Lucian offer astonishingly close indications of the kind of material available to Apuleius.

More important than speculation on the provenance of the individual stories is appreciation of the extraordinary transformation in purpose and tone achieved by Apuleius. The *Onos* reveals that Photius was wrong to regard the original Greek version as a serious story; though its plot hinges on the follies of curiosity and dabbling in magic, there is no moral censure. It is intended purely as entertainment, and the author concentrates on the erotic, sadistic, humorous and scabrous elements. Apuleius at the outset gives the impression that his treatment will be little different. Lucius promises stories told in the language of Miletus, which suggests a volume of risqué escapades after the manner of Aristides; and he offers to soothe the reader's friendly ear with 'elegant whispering'. 'Reader, please concentrate; you'll be delighted.' This programmatic promise, introduced to beguile and deceive, has lulled scholars innocent of Apuleius' evangelical enthusiasms into a false security. Below the sweetness of the fictions lies the usefulness of the message; the parallel with Rabelais' *Gargantua and Pantagruel* is striking. The *Metamorphoses* does not merely expand the original by incorporating a novel medley of spooky, bawdy and sentimental stories; it is also subtly articulated to become a fable with a religious moral.

The hero Lucius, who boasts Plutarch among his forebears, is a youth of good family and liberal education who is impelled by uncontrolled curiosity to seek knowledge of the world of magic through a casual sexual relationship. The anecdotes and additional episodes are artfully aligned to underline his culpability. *En route* to Hypata Aristomenes tells Lucius of the history of Socrates, who forgetful of his family bound himself sexually to Meroe the witch; this is the first warning against the combination of sorcery and sex. At Hypata, a meeting with Lucius' kinswoman Byrrhaena (who again recalls the connexion with Plutarch) reinforces the warning; the statuary in her house depicts the metamorphosis of Actaeon as punishment for curiosity, and Byrrhaena's warning against the witch Pamphile significantly echoes Aristomenes' description of Meroe. In spite of these cautions, Lucius rushes 'like a madman' to satisfy his curiosity by way of Photis the slave-girl's bed, 'however unsafe it proves to be'. Photis adds her ambivalent warning, and at Milo's dinner-table the flickering lamp and (ironically) Lucius' own story of the seer Diophanes should also have given him pause. At the dinner given by Byrrhaena Thelyphron appends his witness; he was a brash visitor to Hypata, like Lucius, and he suffered through underrating the malevolent powers of witches. Finally Lucius undergoes the humiliation of the mock-trial; he thinks he has killed three footpads on his drunken return to Milo's house, whereas he had merely perforated the inflated wineskins exemplifying Pamphile's powers as magician. None of these experiences deters the wilful curiosity of Lucius, with the resultant punishment that he changes himself into an ass.

The two main anecdotes in this section, told by Aristomenes and Thely-phron, are each an ingenious patchwork of different tales stitched together by the professional collector. In themselves they can be criticized for minor inconsistencies, but in their function as indicators of Lucius' weaknesses and as creators of the Hypatan atmosphere of malevolent magic they are most felicitous. But what was the precise nature of Lucius' fault indicated by these warnings? Critics are agreed that the *unhealthy* curiosity for knowledge through magic is central; the proper way to attain knowledge of God and the cosmos, to bridge the chasm between the human and the divine, is not by magic but by the healthy curiosity of study and meditation, a lesson which Plutarch's descendant should not have had to learn. But was the preliminary sexual romp also culpable? The exchanges with Photis are told with such verve that some critics discount sexual culpability. Yet Socrates, the primary *exemplum*, is reprehended for this fault, and in the final book the priest of Isis tells Lucius that his sufferings have been the 'unhappy price for unpropitious curiosity after your descent to slavish pleasures'. Lucius himself confesses the evil errors (*malis erroribus*) of his entanglement with Photis. We should be concerned here not with ancient attitudes in general to such sexual relationships but with the Platonist preoccupations of our author, who in a key passage of the *Apology* (12.1–5) distinguishes the true love of the few from the enslaved passions of beasts and mankind at large. Lucius' sin was chiefly curiosity but also lasciviousness.

The sufferings consequent upon this sinning follow the general pattern of the *Onos*. Of the two sections the first, played against the backcloth of the robbers' hideout, demonstrates the essential ambivalence of the novel. On the one hand the trinity of bandits' stories is recounted in a mock-serious tone undercutting the savagery of Lucius' experiences and encouraging the reader to interpret the romance as light-hearted escapism; on the other, the *conte* of Cupid and Psyche adds a mythological dimension to the serious theme of the romance. Artistically inserted at the heart of the book by Apuleius himself, it presents the experiences of Psyche in parallel with those of Lucius.

Versions of the folk-tale of the bride forbidden to gaze on her husband, who departs in anger when she breaks the taboo and whom she then seeks forlornly through the world, becoming reunited with him only after surmounting apparently impossible tasks imposed by a witch, were already widespread in Apuleius' day; a known North African variant is of particular interest. But no written version incorporating Cupid and Psyche as protagonists predates Apuleius. The likelihood is that our Platonist philosopher has created the story of the marriage, separation and reunification of the god of love and the maiden symbolizing the soul by fusing a version of the folk-tale with a developing motif of literature and art; for the poetry and sculpture of the Alexandrian age exploit that love of Eros and Psyche rooted in the *Phaedrus* and *Symposium*, the dialogues in which Plato depicts the attraction of the soul to the divine by the power of love.

Apuleius shapes the story round the naive curiosity of the ingenuous Psyche, whose jealous sisters plot her downfall. Though urgently warned by Cupid against such 'sacrilegious curiosity', she is persuaded to gaze on the sleeping form of her husband. The oil which in her agitation she spills from the lamp wakes him, and he flies away. Already pregnant, she sunders herself from earthly attachments by contriving the deaths of her sisters, and surrenders herself to the trials of Venus. The last of these is a journey to Proserpina in Hades, from whom she brings a box not to be opened; her 'rash curiosity' in disobeying this injunction renders her insensible, but Cupid rescues her. The child of their marriage in heaven is Voluptas. As Lucius listens to this story told to Charite, he hears without understanding his own history and his future deliverance. He too had been seduced by curiosity, and he too endures the weary pilgrimage, but Isis is to rescue him as Cupid rescues Psyche. He too will undertake a visit to Hades within the symbolism of the Egyptian mysteries, and the fruit of his mystical union with Isis will be *inexplicabilis uoluptas*, a pleasure which cannot be unfolded. Book 11 contains repeated echoes of the story of Psyche to underline that Lucius' relationship with Isis after his wanderings symbolically re-enacts the apotheosis of Psyche.

In the second section of Lucius' sufferings, in which the sequence of peripatetic experiences described in the *Onos* is retained, each adventure is presented as a facet of the degenerate world into which Lucius is plunged. For example, Apuleius enlarges the account of the ass's sufferings at the hands of the cruel boy to superimpose the final laceration of the boy by a bear, thus intensifying the sense of meaningless violence in the world. The radical change introduced to the story of Charite's death (accidental drowning in the original) illustrates the destructive madness induced by Thrasyllus' lust. When Lucius is sold to the eunuch-priests, the hazards experienced in their company from the hostility of both natural and supernatural forces are explored in a trinity of weird stories, and the debased religion of his masters is a further aspect of the corrupt world. The donkey's experiences with later owners repeatedly incorporate anecdotes of sexual promiscuity and destructive magic, themes of particular significance in Lucius' own history; the malevolence of Fortune is a recurring motif throughout, for those whose vision is bounded by the material world are subject to her arbitrary cruelties. But the tone is not one of unrelieved gloom. The artful ambivalence of comedy alternating with the sense of eery, irrational cruelty in the world continues.

Lucius finds his deliverance at the harbour of Cenchreae, a suburb of Corinth. Apuleius may have chosen this locale to achieve an effective contrast between a traditionally dissolute city and the purity of the Isiac regimen; more probably, however, his motive was a desire to describe a centre of Isiac worship with which he was personally acquainted. The existence of a temple to Isis at Cenchreae (and two others at Corinth) is attested by Pausanias and confirmed by archaeological discoveries. The novel now assumes an increasingly auto-biographical flavour. In its final scene at Rome the hero, hitherto a Corinthian, refers to himself as a native of Madauros, the provenance of Apuleius himself. Though attempts have been made to explain away this embarrassing change of *patria*, scholars have usually concluded that the device is adopted to allow Apuleius to present a personal testament. In this final book there is no action beyond Lucius' reversion to human shape and his subsequent initiations; there is little dialogue or interplay with other characters. The exalted narrative is punctuated only by the occasional prayer or sermon. Thus the romance which initially masquerades as titillating entertainment and which unfolds as fable ends on an unabashed note of resounding apologetics, wholly contrasting in tone with the lighter touch of all that precedes.

So the initial prayer of Lucius proclaims Isis as the universal principle of female deity. The description of her appearance in the ensuing vision closely approximates to the iconography of the goddess, and her words exploit an aretalogy to indicate the range of her power and concern and her claim on Lucius' future life. This didactic presentation continues with the detailed description of the ritual and participants in the *Navigium Isidis*, in the course of which Lucius' resumption of human shape provides an occasion for hymning Isis' power afresh. The priest's review of Lucius' sinning and suffering carefully explains the role of Isis as 'the Fortune with eyes', service to whom is true liberty. The description of the temple-ritual incorporates protestations of loyalty to the Roman imperial system. There is an outline of the initiation-ceremony, followed by Lucius' prayer of thanksgiving and praise. The mere catalogue of the content of the final book disposes of the simplistic view that it is nothing more than a final marvel to round off the sequence of weird adventures. The explicit account of the Isiac theology, ritual and observance, recounted with none of the puckish exuberance marking the earlier adventures, is a teaching exercise, a recommendation of the Egyptian religion to a Roman audience. It is legitimate to speculate that it is occasioned by the meteoric growth of contemporary Christianity in North Africa as attested in the writings of Tertullian.

Such a judgement of the nature and purpose of the romance is supported by most modern critics through visualizing the author in the round. The *Apology* delineates the distinction between pursuit of the occult and genuine religious meditation, a distinction which is a central concern of the novel; but the essential key to its psychology resides in the attempt by Middle Platonists to reconcile their philosophy with the religious ideas of the Egyptians, and Plutarch's *De Iside et Osiride* is the most valuable testimony of this.

This treatise explains how and why the cult of Isis and Osiris is worthy of the Platonist's adhesion, and Apuleius' acceptance of the thesis is manifest in both *Apology* and *Florida*. It also offers a clue to the Platonist–Isiac interpretation of the ass-story, which probably originated in Egypt. Plutarch explains that in the dualistic system of Egyptian belief the ass resembles and is controlled by the Satanic principle of evil, Typhon. When Lucius is turned into an ass through magical practices he passes into the dominion of Typhon; and the completely new climax introduced to the novel, by which Apuleius following the example of Xenophon of Ephesus introduces the saving hand of Isis, provides an appropriate deliverance for an asinine Lucius enslaved by Typhon.

How far should this Platonist–Isiac interpretation be pressed? The romance begins with the request of Lucius to the reader 'not to disdain to inspect the Egyptian papyrus inscribed with the subtlety of the Nile reed', and this statement certainly invites symbolic interpretation. But two controlling factors counsel against excesses. The first is the fact that Apuleius follows closely the *Graecanica fabula*, which militates against detailed allegory; secondly, he writes for a lay readership immune from arcane allusion. The main lines of the story could be profitably exploited by the Middle Platonist. In addition to Isiac interpretation of the donkey's career, there is the condemnation of magical practices which becomes more comprehensible in the light of the theory of demonology outlined in *De deo Socratis*, and the animadversions on lust and greed which reflect a central preoccupation of Plato. Moreover, details and motifs introduced into the romance indicate Platonist–Isiac connexions, as when the Egyptian priest Zatchlas appears in the Thelyphron story, or again when Lucius' horse Candidus, implicitly contrasted with the tawny ass of Typhon and evoking the white steed of the tripartite soul in the *Phaedrus*, turns up quite superfluously in the final book. But to interpret the whole romance as a coded aretalogy strains all credibility. Photis is a most improbable 'mystagogic-allegorical figure' antithetic to the true light of Isis; and again the aedile Pythias' command to the vendor to jump on Lucius' fish in the market seems impossibly recondite as an indication of a religious attitude. Similarly the story of Psyche can be generally accepted as Platonist allegory of the progress of the soul, with allusions to the Isiac initiation in the final book, but the suggestion that every detail is invested with mystological significance fails to persuade because the folk-tale cannot sustain such a close-knit interpretation, and even if it could Apuleius' intended readers would have failed to comprehend it.

The characterization in the novel firmly subserves its purpose. Lucius inevitably has a static role. As a man he learns nothing, and becomes an ass; as an ass he evinces no moral progress (how could he?), and his rescue is attributable to an impulsive prayer. Photis (her name is derived from the Greek for 'light', so she is contrapuntal to Lucius, derived from *lux*) is more romantically and sentimentally depicted than is Palaestra ('Wrestling-arena'), the slave-girl of the original. Milo is more miserly, Pamphile ('Love-all') more horrific than their counterparts in the Greek romance. The characters in the inserted anecdotes (their names usually by etymology or historical association indicate their role, sometimes ironically) are frequently inconsistently drawn, partly because Apuleius takes pleasure in welding together different tales, partly because his main effort goes into the alignment of the anecdote with the main plot. So, for example, the widow in the story of Thelyphron, the stepmother in the 'Phaedra' tale (10.2ff.), the female criminal (10.23ff.) all undergo implausible changes of character.

The audience envisaged by Apuleius was one of highly educated Romans. As in Petronius the texture of the story can be highly literary, evoking a wide range of Greek and Latin authors for the pleasure of sophisticated readers. Psyche, for example, not only recalls by her appearance the heroines of the Greek love-romances but also by the nature of her wanderings reincarnates the Io of Aeschylus' dramas, and in her progress through Hades evokes the similar journey of Aeneas. The literary model for Charite's psychological anguish as she prepares suicide is Virgil's Dido. There are scenes in which the more histrionic aspects of forensic speeches are parodied for comic effect, as in the 'trial' at the Festival of Laughter, and again in the speech by the cruel boy's mother after his death (7.27). The novel abounds also in legal quips and jocose references to the activities and interests of the senatorial class at Rome.

The style of the *Metamorphoses*, paralleled in parts of the *Florida* and *De deo Socratis*, is profitably analysed in the company of Fronto and Gellius. The studied artificiality and verbal extravagance which mark all three are not attributable to a peculiar African tradition (though Apuleius' trilingualism in Punic, Greek, and Latin may have fostered a tendency towards exotic diction) but rather to the epideictic tendencies of the Second Sophistic. The *elocutio nouella* associated with the three writers consists of the artistic collocation of words of arresting novelty – a combination of archaisms and Graecisms, vulgarisms and neologisms. The language of comedy is frequently exploited in dialogue, especially where the homely, old-fashioned flavour is apposite to the characters. Occasionally the etymological sense of a word is restored with bizarre effect; Cupid, for example, is not only *inuisus* ('unseen') but also *inhumanus* ('divine'). The influence of Asianic oratory, so marked in the Greek novels of Achilles Tatius and Longus, is even stronger in Apuleius, inspiring the rhythmical, rhyming riots of double, triple and quadruple phrases and clauses, consummately balanced by isocolon, homoioteleuton, alliteration, and assonance.

The influence of Apuleius' novel on European literature since the Italian Renaissance has been profound. Boccaccio helped to popularize it by transcribing the Monte Cassino manuscript with his own hand. Within fifty years of the invention of printing, editions had appeared in several Italian cities and at Paris, and the sixteenth century introduced influential translations in Italian, Spanish, French, German and English. Apuleius was the most powerful single influence at the birth of the picaresque novel in Spain; *Laʒarillo de Tormes*, Alemán's *Guʒmán*, Úbeda's *La pícara Justina* and other early works of fiction appropriate incidents from the *Metamorphoses* which are told by the peripatetic servant in the I-narrative with frequent allusions to the asinine forbear. *Cupid and Psyche* has its own distinguished history at the hands of Boccaccio, Calderón, La Fontaine, Heywood, Beaumont, Marmion, to name only a few. Many of Apuleius' ironical anecdotes are incorporated in Italian and French collections of such tales. Finally, the florid, ornamental texture of Apuleius' language had its imitators in the Euphuistic romances of Lyly and his successors.

# EPILOGUE

The primary aim of any literary history is to foster a deeper appreciation of the creative writing which it describes; to define the qualities of the works themselves must be its main concern. Roman literature, however, demands the reader's attention for a second reason, because more than any other national literature it has dictated the forms and modes of thought of subsequent European letters. For more than fifteen centuries after Virgil and Livy, Latin remained the learned language of Europe, constantly evoking the great *auctores* of the classical period. Then, side by side with the Latin writings of the High Middle Ages and the Renaissance, the vernacular literatures of the twelfth to the sixteenth centuries likewise boast their proud descent from the antique Romans, who continue to breathe inspiration into Western letters after the Renaissance. This epilogue concerns itself chiefly with the medieval period and the more important classical influences within it.

The ways in which the Latin classics impinged on the imaginative experience of later generations were shaped by a complex of political, economic and social factors but above all by the emergence of dominant Christian thinkers in the fourth-century West. These Christian leaders, emerging shortly after the establishment of Christianity as the favoured religion of the state, exploited their education in classical eloquence to proclaim the superiority of Christian beliefs over traditional Roman values. As Christians they inherited attitudes towards classical literature in which the denunciation of a Tertullian rang louder than the approval of a Lactantius; as educated Romans they found their modes of thought and powers of expression moulded by the authors they sought to reject. Thus in Africa, Italy, Gaul, Spain an ambivalence towards classical literature is evinced not only in the same milieux but even in the same individuals. The Ambrose who proclaimed that the scriptures contained all necessary instruction was the Ambrose who exploited Cicero's *De officiis* for his *De officiis ministrorum*. The Jerome who asks *quid facit cum Apostolo Cicero?* 'What has Cicero to do with Paul?', is the Jerome whose justification of classical studies elsewhere encourages later churchmen in their pursuit of them. The Paulinus who bids Ausonius reject the pagan Muses and spurns the voices of

Terence and Virgil is the Paulinus who adapts the genres of classical poetry to the proclamation of the Christian message. The Augustine whose *De doctrina Christiana* sponsors the teaching of the liberal arts is the Augustine who later argues against their relevance for the Christian life.

This ambivalence remains characteristic of much Christian thinking throughout the Middle Ages, for clerics are susceptible to the 'humanist' enthusiasm of men like Prudentius and Cassiodorus on the one side, and to the condemnations of those like Gregory the Great ('The same lips cannot sound the praises of both Jupiter and Christ') on the other. Even Alcuin, whose verses so often evoke Virgil and who is known by the soubriquet Flaccus at Charlemagne's court, can reprimand his monks for enjoying Virgil in private. But by the ninth century the value of classical literature, initially as ancillary to biblical study but increasingly as inculcating higher cultural standards in both state and church, is almost universally recognized.

Utilitarian functions rather than literary qualities dictate the pattern of survival and study of texts up to the Renaissance, as the contents of libraries at York, Corbie and Lorsch demonstrate. Lyric and love-elegy lie below ground; Catullus, Tibullus, Propertius appear only occasionally in a catalogue or isolated quotation, though Horace's *Odes* become popular from the eleventh century, and Ovid's fame is even more widespread subsequently. The fiction of Petronius and Apuleius, irrelevant to Christian education, is ignored till the Renaissance, when Apuleius aids the creation of the Spanish picaresque novel. The letters of Cicero and Pliny remain virtually unread until the fourteenth century. The didactic epic of Lucretius, closely studied by Christian savants like Lactantius and Prudentius, vanishes subsequently till rediscovered by Poggio.

The most pervasive classical genre throughout the medieval period was epic, and the epic poet dominating the millennium was Virgil. Evoked or echoed on almost every page by Prudentius and Paulinus, exploited by practitioners of biblical and courtly epic in the late Empire, allegorized by Fulgentius in the sixth century as by Bernard Silvester in the twelfth, Augustine's *poeta nobilissimus* reaches the summit of his glory in the Carolingian age, the *aetas Vergiliana*. Subsequently, he continues to be the model of epic poets, both Latin and vernacular. Dante signals his supremacy by greeting Virgil as 'lo mio maestro e il mio autore', and the *Aeneid* likewise inspires the epics of Camoens, Tasso and Milton. But if Virgil is the sun, lesser stars of Roman epic twinkle round him. Lucan's colourful style won him regular imitators from Lactantius to the Renaissance, and Dante places him with Homer, Horace and Ovid in the reception-party for Virgil in Hades. Statius' *Thebaid* is another perennial favourite for its flavour of mythological romance and its allegorical mode. Claudian is not continuously popular, but his poetry is familiar especially to twelfth-century *literati*.

Of the epic composed between the ninth and thirteenth centuries, five works stand out proclaiming their debt to classical Roman poetry. *Waltharius*, composed in the late ninth century by the Geraldus cited in the prologue, is a romantic epic which in structure recalls Statius' *Thebaid* and in texture reveals (on occasion with ironical humour) close acquaintance with Virgil. *Ruodlieb*, the German epic of romantic chivalry composed in the eleventh century, incorporates imitations of Virgil and of Virgil's Christian imitator Prudentius. The three other poems signal the range of twelfth-century epic. Alan of Lille's *Anticlaudianus* is a philosophical epic which proclaims a connexion with Claudian's *In Rufinum*, but which in texture effortlessly evokes the whole sweep of Roman epic poets. As mythological epic Joseph of Exeter's *Frigii Daretis Yliados libri sex* likewise contains ubiquitous echoes of Virgil, Lucan, Statius and Claudian. Walter of Châtillon's *Alexandreis* exemplifies historical epic, the versification of Curtius Rufus by a learned poet with echoes of Roman epic at his mind's command.

In this survey of the epic tradition the *Metamorphoses* must not be forgotten, but Ovid merits separate discussion. His virtuosity with the elegiac couplet is widely imitated by Christian versifiers from the fourth to the sixth centuries; Venantius Fortunatus, for example, adapts Ovidian techniques for both polite verse-epistles and religious verses, presenting the great Pauline paradoxes (death to the world as spiritual life, the dead wood of the Cross as a living tree) in the Ovidian manner. Though little read in Ireland and England from the sixth to the eighth centuries, Ovid was a model for composition for learned Carolingians, and during the eleventh to the thirteenth centuries (the *aetas Ovidiana*) became the most influential representative of Roman letters. His role as *magister amoris curialis* 'master of courtly love' begins with the churchmen Marbod, Baudry, and Hildebert, who in verse-epistles and epigrams deploy Ovidian rhythms and tricks of style in essaying chaster themes. Subsequently, in the less inhibited, more secularized twelfth-century France, Ovid is echoed constantly in the classicizing poems and in the rhythmical rhyming verses of medieval lyric – in Hugo of Orléans, in the Archpoet, in Walter of Châtillon, in the numerous collections of anonymous versifiers preserved in such collections as the *Carmina Burana*.

But turn the coin, and the love-practitioner of the *Ars amatoria* and the *Heroides* assumes a more sober demeanour. The myth of creation in the *Metamorphoses* is deployed by Bernard Silvester and his fellow-Chartrians to launch the figure of *Ovidius physicus*. A stream of commentators – Manegold of Lautenbach in the eleventh century, Arnoul of Orléans in the twelfth, John of Garland's *Integumenta Ovidii* in the thirteenth, the vernacular poem *Ovide moralisé* in the fourteenth – allegorizes the *Metamorphoses* to unveil the *Ovidius mythographus*. The *florilegia* which assemble his moral tags are the basis of

*Ovidius ethicus.* Not surprisingly therefore this teacher of physics, ethics, and allegory is depicted as a Christian in the pseudo-Ovidian *De vetula* (c. 1260), and the popular derivation of his name (*Ouidius quasi ouum diuidens, id est occultum reserans* 'Ovid, because he splits the egg, in other words uncovers what is hidden') alludes to him as the fountainhead of knowledge.

Third in importance in medieval influence come the satirists Horace, Persius and Juvenal, perennially popular from the later Empire to the Renaissance both as models for classroom-composition and as critics of human folly. When satire as a genre emerges in the self-critical society of twelfth-century France, this trinity constantly hovers near.

> Flaccus Horatius et Cato, Persius et Iuuenalis
> Quid facerent, rogo, si foret his modo uita sodalis?
> *Horatius Flaccus, Cato, Persius, Juvenal – what would they do, I ask, if they shared the life of today?*

asks Bernard of Cluny in *De contemptu mundi.* The targets of satire are those pilloried by Juvenal and his Christian imitator Jerome – sexual vice, the monstrous regiment of women, gluttony in food and drink, the avarice and meanness of the powerful – but within the changed framework of the Christian ecclesiastical establishment. When Nigel Longchamps in his *Speculum stultorum* and other satirists berate the vices of monks and clerics, Juvenal naturally comes through more loudly than Horace and Persius. But the greatest medieval satirist, Walter of Châtillon, using rhythmical rhyming measures, constantly underpins pungent attacks on his society with evocations of all three. The technique is particularly impressive in poems like *Missus sum in uineam*, where Walter ends each stanza with a line from Horace, Persius, Juvenal, Ovid, or other *auctor.* Martial is another popular model for the satirical epigram of this period.

Pastoral poetry in classical Rome had been dominated by Virgil; flanked by Calpurnius Siculus and Nemesianus (whose work was much studied in the Carolingian age), his *Eclogues* have a curious after-history in which the Arcadian *pastor* and his sheep merge with the ecclesiastical *pastor gregis.* In the Carolingian age, Alcuin's 'cuckoo'-poems are Virgilian pastiche spoken by Virgilian shepherds in description of the life of the palace-school. Sedulius Scottus likewise uses the eclogue-form to describe the circle of bishop Hartgar at Liège. But the most influential ninth-century adaptation of Virgilian pastoral was the *Ecloga Theoduli*, in which the shepherd Pseustis and shepherdess Alithia ('Deceit' and 'Truth') recommend respectively pagan mythology and biblical truth in bucolic contest. In the twelfth century the eclogues of 'M. Valerius', usually regarded merely as literary exercises, are better interpreted as facets of clerical experience in a courtly milieu. The classical formulation of pastoral now exists side by side with the Latin pastourelle which emerges from imitation of Provençal poetry.

The absence of secular drama from the medieval stage spelt neglect of Roman dramatists. Seneca's tragedies had considerable literary influence in the late Roman period, conspicuously in Boethius' *Consolation of philosophy*, in which the verses constantly echo Senecan odes. But subsequently the plays are known only to widely-read scholars, to an Aldhelm in Anglo-Saxon England, to a Eugenius Vulgarius in ninth-century Italy, and later to a Liutprand, a Papias, a Richard de Fourneval. The fame of Seneca comes later with the Italian humanists, the Elizabethan dramatists and with Corneille. Of the comic playwrights, Plautus throughout the Middle Ages remained less known even than Seneca, but by contrast Terence was a favourite author, because of his philosophic reflections on the human condition. Terence inspires the dramas of the tenth-century nun Hrotsvitha, whose six plays on Christian themes reflect in structure and dialogue the influence of the *Andria* and to a lesser degree the *Eunuch* and *Adelphoe*. In the twelfth century Ovidian narrative-comedies become popular, deriving their themes from Plautus and Terence through prose-summaries of the plays. Vitalis of Blois wrote an *Amphitruo* and an *Aulularia*, Matthew of Vendôme a *Miles gloriosus*; an unknown author's *Pamphilus et Gliscerium* derives from the *Andria*. The Renaissance established a vogue for the Roman comic playwrights as for Seneca; translations of their plays, and original Latin plays based on them, were performed in Venice and other Italian cities.

Cicero dominates the study of rhetoric. He was a special favourite of the Christian apologists Lactantius and Jerome, whose seven polemical treatises echo Ciceronian phraseology and techniques. Gradually, however, Cicero's speeches fell out of general currency, though in the Carolingian period the best-read scholars like Sedulius Scottus and Lupus of Ferrières knew one or another of them; Christian eloquence had different objectives. Augustine initiated Christian theory on the art of preaching; epistolary style, extending more generally into rules for artistic prose, became important from the eleventh century: and the theory of poetic composition was also extensively discussed. The bases of instruction for all three were the *De inventione* of Cicero and the *ad Herennium*, known familiarly as *Rhetorica prima* and *Rhetorica secunda*; Horace's *Ars poetica* is also important for poetic theory. The *De inventione* fathers innumerable manuals between the fourth and thirteenth centuries. Of other classical treatises, Cicero's *Brutus* remained unread, but his *De oratore* and Quintilian's *Institutio* were known to the best scholars from Lupus of Ferrières to John of Salisbury, whose contemporary Ulrich of Bamberg remarks: *In rethorica educandus legat primam Tullii rethoricam, et librum ad Herennium, et Tullium de oratore, et causas Quintiliani* [the ps.-Quintilian] *et Quintilianum de oratoris institutione* 'So far as rhetoric goes, the person to be instructed should read the first rhetorical treatise of Cicero, the volume to Herennius, Tully's *On the orator*, the cases of Quintilian and Quintilian's *On the education of the orator*.'

The fate of the classical historians has little relevance to their quality. Tacitus, largely unread in the third century when the emperor of the same name had copies made *ne lectorum incuria deperiret* 'so that the historian should not be lost through the indifference of readers', might have vanished for ever through neglect but for the vigilance of Renaissance humanists. Livy's massive history was epitomized within a century of his death, and the summaries ousted all but the earlier romantic sections of political and martial glory. These early books were studied by scholars of the Carolingian and Ottonian periods, and from the eleventh century appear increasingly in library-catalogues; it is difficult to affirm positively that in the golden age of medieval historiography historians like William of Malmesbury had read Livy, but the general presentation and especially the prominence of the speeches strongly suggest it. But Livy becomes a giant only with the new dawn of Petrarch and Boccaccio, Bruni and Machiavelli. Before the Renaissance only Sallust of the major historians was widely known, being studied for his simpler style and heavier moralizing. He is an important model for historians from the tenth to the twelfth century, such as Richer, William of Poitiers, and the author of *Vita Heinrici IV Imperatoris*. The close imitation of Suetonius' *Vitae* by Einhard's *Life of Charlemagne* was exceptional; the Roman biographer was not widely studied. Caesar too was a neglected author, though known to Bede, Einhard, William of Poitiers and William of Malmesbury. The fact is that Christian historiography has other models for histories of church and people, especially Eusebius, Orosius, and (for biography) Sulpicius Severus.

Popular philosophy as represented by Cicero and Seneca forms a pervasive strand of medieval thought, the vocabulary of which owes much to Ciceronian innovation. Cicero is influential chiefly as transmitter of Hellenistic philosophical ideas to the increasingly Greekless Christians of the west. Augustine's celebrated tribute to the *Hortensius* (now lost) as the work which converted him to philosophy, Macrobius' commentary on the *Somnium Scipionis*, Boethius' interest in Ciceronian logic exemplify different facets of his influence in late antiquity, but the chief importance of Cicero as of Seneca lies in the formulation of Stoic ethical ideas, much of which graduated into Christian moral theology. At the apogee of medieval philosophy, thinkers from Abélard to Aquinas repeatedly signal their respect for the two pagan *auctores*. For Abélard, Cicero is *maximus philosophorum latinorum* 'the greatest of the Latin philosophers', and Seneca *summus inter uniuersos philosophos morum praedicator* 'the greatest of all philosophers as a preacher of manners'. The psychological and ethical sections of Aquinas' *Summa theologiae*, which attempt to reconcile the re-emergent Aristotle with the traditional Stoic–Christian position, repeatedly quote from the *Tusculans* and from the *De officiis*, which was the main source for ancient ethical theory till Aristotle was rediscovered. The *De amicitia* is another seminal work of Cicero, repeatedly quoted in treatises on human and divine love. Though no scholar before William of Malmesbury knew the entire corpus of Seneca's *Moral epistles*, his work was studied in more restricted compass in the schools and the monasteries, and the *Quaestiones naturales* inspired a treatise of the same title by Adelard of Bath.

This brief sketch reveals how vital the study of the classical authors is for a thorough understanding of the central intellectual concerns of the Middle Ages. The scholar who carries forward his knowledge of the Roman authors, and complements this secular learning with a knowledge of the Latin Bible and the Fathers, will have the indispensable tools for an understanding of medieval literature.

# APPENDIX OF
# AUTHORS AND WORKS

## THE LATER PRINCIPATE

### GENERAL WORKS

(1) History of late antiquity

Bury, J. B., *History of the later Roman empire from the death of Theodosius I to the death of Justinian* (repr. London 1958).

Jones, A. H. M., *The later Roman empire*, 3 vols. (Oxford 1964; with maps).

Lot, F., *The end of the ancient world and the beginning of the middle ages* (New York 1932).

Mazzarino, S., *The end of the ancient world* (London 1966).

Rémondon, R., *La crise de l'empire romain: de Marc-Aurèle à Anastase* (Paris 1964).

Stein, E., *Histoire du bas-empire I: de l'état romain à l'état byzantin* (Paris 1959).

Walbank, F. W., *The awful revolution: the decline of the Roman empire in the West* (Liverpool 1969).

(2) Culture, religion and art

*Entretiens XXIII: Christianisme et formes littéraires de l'antiquité tardive en occident* (Fondation Hardt, Geneva 1977).

Bowder, D. *The age of Constantine and Julian* (London 1978).

Brown, P. R. L., *The world of late antiquity* (London 1971).

idem, *Religion and society in the age of St. Augustine* (London 1972).

Courcelle, P., *Late Latin writers and their Greek sources* (Cambridge, Mass. 1969).

Dodds, E. R., *Pagan and Christian in an age of anxiety* (Cambridge 1965).

Geffcken, J., *The last days of Greco-Roman paganism* (Amsterdam 1978).

Glover, T. R., *Life and letters in the fourth century* (Cambridge 1961).

Grabar, A., *The beginnings of Christian art, 200–395* (London 1967).

Marrou, H.-I., *Décadence romaine ou antiquité tardive? IIIe–IVe siècle* (Paris 1977).

Momigliano, A. D. (ed.), *The conflict between paganism and Christianity* (Oxford 1963).

Paschoud, F., *Roma aeterna: études sur le patriotisme romain dans l'occident latin à l'époque des grandes invasions* (Rome–Geneva 1967) 133–55.

Vogt, J., *The decline of Rome* (London 1967).

# ANNIANUS, SEPTIMIUS SEVERUS, etc.

TEXT: E. Castorina, *I poetae novelli* (Florence 1941).

# HADRIAN

TEXT: *FPL* 136.

# NEMESIANUS, MARCUS AURELIUS OLYMPIUS

## LIFE AND WORKS

Late 3rd c. A.D., from Carthage. Author of four *Eclogues*, once ascribed to Calpurnius (see M. Haupt, *De carminibus bucolicis Calpurnii et Nemesiani* (Berlin 1854)); *Cynegetica* (written *c.* 284, see vv. 63–5; 325 lines survive); and perhaps of two fragments *De aucupio*. Also wrote on fishing and sailing (*Hist. Aug. Carinus* 11.2) and projected an epic on Carinus and Numerianus (*Cyn.* 63–5).

## BIBLIOGRAPHY

TEXTS: P. van der Woestijne (Bruges 1937); C. Giarratano, 3rd ed. (Turin 1943); P. Vopilhac (Budé, 1975).
STUDIES: J. Meurice, *Essai sur les Bucoliques de Némésien* (Liege 1935); W. Schmid, 'Tityrus Christianus', *Rh.M.* 96 (1953) 101–65; B. Luiselli, 'Il proemio del Cynegeticon di Olimpio Nemesiano', *S.I.F.C.* 30 (1958) 73–95.

# REPOSIANUS

TEXT: *Anth. Lat.* 253; *PLM* IV 348ff.; U. Zuccarelli (Naples 1972).

STUDIES: J. Tolkiehn, 'Das Gedicht des Reposianus', *Jh.f.Kl.Phil.* 155 (1897) 615ff.; U. Zuccarelli, *Lessico di Reposiano* (Naples 1976).

# PENTADIUS

TEXT: *Anth. Lat.* 234–5, 265–8; *PLM* IV 343–6, 358–9.

# EPISTULA DIDONIS

TEXT: *Anth. Lat.* 83; *PLM* IV 271–7.

# VESPA

TEXTS AND COMMENTARY TEXT: *Anth. Lat.* 199; *PLM* IV 326–30. COMMENTARY: F. Pini (Rome 1958: with tr.).

STUDIES: O. Weinreich, 'Zu Vespas iudicium coci et pistoris', *Hermes* 50 (1915) 315f.; V. Tandoi, 'Il contrasto del cuoco e del fornaio', *A. & R.* n.s.4 (1959) 198–215.

# VERBA ACHILLIS IN PARTHENONE

TEXT: *Anth. Lat.* 198; *PLM* IV 322–5.

# PERVIGILIUM VENERIS

Poem in ninety-three trochaic verses celebrating spring and the forthcoming festival of Venus; date and author unknown. Location of festival, v. 49: '*iussit Hyblaeis tribunae stare diua floribus*'. Of the three Sicilian cities called Hybla (Steph. Byz. s.v.) the reference is probably to Hybla Gereatis on the slopes of Etna, the modern Paterno, twelve miles west of Catania. Cf. Schilling *ad* v. 49.

### BIBLIOGRAPHY

TEXT: R. Schilling (Budé, 1944: with brief notes).

TRANSLATION: J. Lindsay, *Song of a falling world* (London 1948) 64–8.

STUDIES: E. K. Rand, 'Sur le Pervigilium Veneris', *R.E.L.* 12 (1934) 83–95; P. Boyancé, 'Encore le Pervigilium Veneris', *R.E.L.* 28 (1950) 212–35; I. Cazzaniga, 'Saggio critico ed esegetico intorno al Pervigilium Veneris', *S.C.O.* 2 (1953) 47–101.

# DISTICHA CATONIS

TEXT: M. Boas (Amsterdam 1952); *PLM* III 205–42.

STUDIES: F. Skutsch, *RE* V (1905) 358–70.

# OPTATIANUS PORFYRIUS, PUBLILIUS

## LIFE AND WORKS

Early 4th c. A.D., probably an African and to be identified with the *Praefectus urbi* in 329 and 333. Author of a collection of poems in acrostic and other highly contrived forms. Nos. 1–20 form part of a panegyric sent to Constantine 325/326. Sources: Optatianus 2.31; Jerome, *Chron.* A.D. 328; letter of Constantine quoted in prose preface to O.'s poems. Cf. *PLRE* I 649.

TEXTS AND COMMENTARY: TEXTS: L. Müller (BT, 1877); E. Kluge (BT, 1926). COMMENTARY: G. Polara, 2 vols. (Turin 1973).

# TIBERIANUS

## LIFE

Praetorian Prefect in Gaul A.D. 336–7 (Jerome, *Chron.* A.D. 335); earlier appointments in Africa and Spain (*Cod. Theod.* 3.5.6, 12.5.1; *Cod. Iust.* 6.1.6).

## WORKS

Twenty trochaic tetrameters catalectic (*Amnis ibat*); twenty-eight hexameters on the evils of gold (attributed to T. by Serv. *ad Aen.* 6.136); other fragments preserved by Serv. *ad Aen.* 6.532, Fulg. *Myth.* 3.7 and *Expos. serm.* s.v. *sudum*.

## BIBLIOGRAPHY

TEXT: *PLM* III 263–9.

TRANSLATION: J. Lindsay, *Song of a falling world* (London 1948) 61–4.

STUDIES: H. Lewy, 'A Latin hymn to the creator ascribed to Plato', *H.Th.R.* 31 (1946) 243–88; E. R. Curtius, *European literature and the Latin middle ages*, tr. W. R. Trask (London 1953) 196–200.

# [LACTANTIUS], DE AVE PHOENICE

TEXT: *PLM* III 247–62; *Anth. Lat.* 731.

# IUVENCUS, GAIUS VETTIUS AQUILINUS

## LIFE AND WORKS

Spanish priest, fl. under Constantine. *Evangeliorum libri IV*: hexameter narrative of the gospel story. Sources: Jerome, *Chron.* A.D. 328, *De vir. ill.* 84; Juvencus 4.805.

## BIBLIOGRAPHY

TEXT: J. Huemer, *CSEL* XXIV (Vienna 1891).

STUDIES: C. Wegman, 'Zu Iuvencus', *Beiträge zur Geschichte der christlich-lateinischen Poesie* (Munich 1926) 21–8; U. Moricca, *Studi di letteratura latina cristiana* II.2 (Turin 1928) 831ff.; H. H. Kievits, *Ad Iuvenci evangeliorum librum primum commentarius exegeticus* (Groningen 1940); J. de Wit, *Ad Iuvenci evangeliorum librum secundum commentarius exegeticus* (Groningen 1947); N. Hannson, *Textkritische zu Iuvencus, mit vollständigem Index verborum* (Lund 1950); R. Herzog, *Die Bibelepik der lateinischen Spätantike* I (Munich 1972) esp. 52–98.

# AVIENIUS, POSTUMIUS RUFIUS FESTUS

## LIFE

4th c. A.D. from Volsinii in Etruria.

## WORKS

*Descriptio orbis terrae*: geography in hexameters based on Greek original by Dionysius Periegetes. *Ora maritima*: description in iambics of western and southern coasts of Europe (see 51ff.), written after *Descriptio* (*Ora mar.* 71); section on coast from Marseilles to Cadiz alone survives. *Aratea, Phaenomena* and *Prognostica*: expanded hexameter translations of Aratus. Sources: *CIL* VI 537 (= *ILS* 2944); *IG* III 635; inscription from Bulla Regia (*PLRE* I 336); Jerome, *In ep. ad Tit.* 1.12; Serv. *ad Aen.* 10.272 and 388 (poem on Virgilian legends and iambic epitome of Livy, possibly by Avianus).

## BIBLIOGRAPHY

TEXTS AND COMMENTARIES: TEXTS: A. Holder (Innsbruck 1887). *Descriptio*: P. van de Woestijne (Bruges 1961). COMMENTARIES: *Ora maritima*: A. Schulten (Barcelona–Berlin 1922); A. Berthelot (Paris 1934).

STUDIES: J. F. Matthews, 'Continuity in a Roman family: the Festi of Volsinii', *Historia* 16 (1967) 484–09; A. Cameron, 'Macrobius, Avienus and Avianus', *C.Q.* n.s. 17 (1967) 385–99.

# AUSONIUS, DECIMUS MAGNUS

## LIFE

b. in Bordeaux A.D. 310. Taught there for thirty years, then summoned by Valentinian to be tutor to Gratian; joined them in campaigns in Germany 368–9. Praetorian Prefect in Gaul 378 and consul 379. On Gratian's murder in 383 retired to Bordeaux and d. 393/394. Sources: Auson. *praef.*; Symm. *Epist.* 1.13–43, 1.20, 22, 23; Auson. *Grat. act.* 2.11, 8.40; Auson. *Epist.* 27.90ff., 31.

## WORKS

Following are likely dates of composition for those of A.'s works whose chronology can be established; few if any of them are certain. (Page refs. to Peiper's ed.) *c.* 335: *Epistula ad patrem de suscepto filio* (p. 255). 367–371: *Versus Paschales* (p. 17). 368: *Cento nuptialis* (p. 206). 369: *Bissula* poems (p. 114). 370–371: *Mosella* (p. 118), *Epist.* 4, 6, 7 (p. 232). 374: *Epist.* 12 (p. 238). 378–379: *Epicedion in patrem* (p. 21), *Precationes* (p. 24). 379: *Gratiarum actio* (p. 353), *Epist.* 11 (p. 236), *De herediolo* (p. 16), *Ordo urbium nobilium* (? 1st ed.; p. 144). 380: *Caesares* (p. 183), *Epist.* 2 (p. 222). 379–383: *Parentalia* (p. 28), *Epist.* 23, 25, 26 (p. 268). 383: *Technopaegnion* (p. 155). 380–389: *Commemoratio professorum Burdigalensium* (p. 48). 388–390: *Ordo urbium nobilium* (p. 144). 389–390: *Epitaphia* (p. 72). 390: *Ludus septem sapientium* (p. 169). Arguments on dating of A.'s poems are most clearly set out in Pastorino's ed., intr. 70–105. Cf. *PLRE* I 140–1.

### BIBLIOGRAPHY

TEXTS AND COMMENTARIES: TEXTS: K. Schenkl (Berlin 1883); R. Peiper (BT, 1886); H. G. Evelyn White (Loeb, 1919); A. Pastorino (Turin 1971); S. Prete (BT, 1978). COMMENTARIES: *Mosella*: C. Hosius, 3rd ed. (Marburg 1926); W. John (Trier 1932); E. H. Blakeney (London 1933); A. Marsili (Turin 1957).

TRANSLATION: J. Lindsay, *Song of a falling world* (London 1948) 70–82 (select poems).

STUDIES: R. Pichon, *Les derniers écrivains profanes* (Paris 1906) 151–216, 297–319; A. Delachaux, *La latinité d'Ausone* (Neuchâtel 1909); S. Dill, *Roman society in the last century of the western empire*, 2nd ed. (London 1910) 167–86; J. M. Byrne, *Prolegomena to an edition of the works of Decimus Magnus Ausonius* (New York 1916); M. J. Pattist, *Ausonius als Christ* (Amsterdam 1925); Z. A. A. Jouai, *De magistraat Ausonius* (Nijmegen 1938); N. K. Chadwick, *Poetry and letters in early Christian Gaul* (London 1955) 47–62; S. Prete, *Ricerche sulla storia del testo di Ausonio* (Rome 1960); M. K. Hopkins, 'Social mobility in the later Roman empire. The evidence of Ausonius', *C.Q.* n.s.11 (1961) 239–49; A. Pastorino, 'A proposito della tradizione del testo di Ausonio', *Maia* 14 (1962) 41–68, 212–43; D. Korzeniewski, 'Aufbau und Struktur der Mosella des Ausonius', *Rh.M.* 106 (1963) 80–95; P. Courcelle, *Histoire littéraire des grandes invasions germaniques*, 3rd ed. (Paris 1964) 293–302.

# EPIGRAMMATA BOBBIENSIA

On Naucellius, see Symm. *Epist.* 3.10–16; *Epigr. Bobb.* 2–4, 7; *PLRE* I 617–18.

TEXTS: F. Munari (Rome 1955); W. Speyer (BT 1963).

STUDIES: W. Speyer, *Naucellius und sein Kreis* (Munich 1959), reviewed by W. Schmid, *Gnomon* 32 (1960) 340–60; S. Mariotti, *RE* suppl. IX (1962) 37–64.

# CLAUDIANUS, CLAUDIUS

## LIFE

b. *c.* A.D. 370 in Alexandria. Came to Rome *c.* 394 and became court poet under Honorius and his regent Stilicho. After moving to Milan (where he obtained senatorial status), returned to Rome in 400 and was honoured with a statue for his panegyric on Stilicho's consulate; in the same year married a noble African through influence of Stilicho's wife Serena. Probably d. in Rome 404. Sources: *CIL* VI 1710 ( = *ILS* 2949) (honours); Suda s.v. Κλαυδιανὸς Ἀλεξανδριεύς; Claud. *Carm.* 39.20 (native of Alexandria), 42.14 (arrival in Rome); August. *C.D.* 5.26, Oros. 7.35 (religion).

## WORKS

1: *In consulatum Olybrii et Probini* (395). 2–5: *In Rufinum* (395). 6–7: *De III consulatu Honorii Augusti* (396). 8: *De IV consulatu Honorii Augusti* (398). 9–10: *De nuptiis Honorii et Mariae* (398). 11–14: *Fescennina* (398). 15: *De bello Gildonico* (398). 16–17: *De consulatu Manlii Theodori* (399). 18–20: *In Eutropium* (399–400). 21–4: *De consulatu Stilichonis* (399–400). 25–6: *De bello Pollentino* (402). 27–8: *De VI consulatu Honorii Augusti* (404). 29: *Laus Serenae* (?404). Unfinished epic *De raptu Proserpinae* and remaining poems not datable with certainty.

## BIBLIOGRAPHY

TEXTS AND COMMENTARIES: TEXTS: T. Birt (Berlin 1892); J. Koch (BT, 1893); M. Platnauer (Loeb, 1922), COMMENTARIES: *De raptu Proserpinae*: J. B. Hall (Cambridge 1969). *In Rufinum*: H. L. Levy (Detroit 1971). *De IV consulatu Honorii*: P. Fargues (Aix-en-Provence 1936). *De nuptiis Honorii et Mariae*: U. Frings (Meisenheim am Glan 1975). *De bello Gildonico*: M. E. Olechowska (Leiden 1978). *De consulatu Manlii Theodori*: W. Simon (Berlin 1975). *In Eutropium*: P. Fargues (Paris 1933). *De bello Pallentino*: H. Schroff (Berlin 1927). *De VI consulatu Honorii*: K. A. Müller (Berlin 1938).

TRANSLATION: J. Lindsay, *Song of a falling world* (London 1948) 135–60 (selections).

STUDIES: P. Fargues, *Claudien: études sur sa poésie et son temps* (Paris 1933); T. Nissen, 'Historisches Epos und Panegyrikus in der Spätantike', *Hermes* 75 (1940) 298–325; N. Martinelli, 'Saggio sui carmi greci di Claudiano', *Miscellanea Galbiati II*

(Rome 1957) 47–76; D. Romano, *Claudiano* (Palermo 1958); F. Paschoud, *Roma aeterna: études sur le patriotisme romain dans l'occident latin à l'époque des grandes invasions* (Rome–Geneva 1967) 133–55; A. Gualandri, *Aspetti della tecnica compositiva in Claudiano* (Milan 1969); P. G. Christiansen, *The use of images by Claudius Claudianus* (The Hague 1969); A. Cameron, *Claudian. Poetry and propaganda at the court of Honorius* (Oxford 1970); U. Keudel, *Poetische Vorläufer und Vorbilder in Claudians De consulatu Stilichonis* (Göttingen 1970); A. Cameron, 'Claudian', in (ed.) J. W. Binns, *Latin literature of the fourth century* (London 1974) 134–59.

# PRUDENTIUS CLEMENS, AURELIUS

## LIFE

b. A.D. 348 in Hispania Tarraconensis. Gave up a successful public career (provincial governorship, high office under Theodosius) to devote himself to writing Christian poetry. Sources: Prud. *praef.*; Gennadius, *De vir. ill.* 13.

## WORKS

(1) IN LYRIC METRES: *Cathemerinon*: twelve hymns. *Peristephanon*: fourteen poems in praise of Christian martyrs. (2) IN HEXAMETERS: *Apotheosis*: on the doctrine of the Trinity. *Hamartigeneia*: on the origin of sin. *Psychomachia*: allegory on the Christian virtues and pagan vices. *Contra Symmachum*: polemic against paganism in two books. *Dittochaeon*: on scriptural subjects from both testaments. Pubd together in 404 (Prud. *praef.* 1). Cf. *praef.* 34–42 (list of works, possibly chronological) and *PLRE* I 214.

## BIBLIOGRAPHY

TEXTS AND COMMENTARY: TEXTS: J. Bergman, *CSEL* LXI (Vienna 1926); M. Lavarenne (Budé, 1943–51); H. J. Thomson (Loeb, 1949–53).; M. P. Cunningham, *CC* CXXVI (Turnhout 1966). COMMENTARY: *Cathemerinon* 1, 2, 5 and 6: M. M. Hijmans-van Assendelft (Groningen 1976).

TRANSLATION: J. Lindsay, *Song of a falling world* (London 1948) 96–106 (select poems).

STUDIES: I. Rodriguez-Herrera, *Poeta Christianus: Prudentius' Auffassung vom Wesen und von der Aufgabe des christlichen Dichters* (Speyer 1936); B. Peebles, *The poet Prudentius* (New York 1951); M. Lavarenne, *Études sur la langue du poète Prudence* (Paris 1953); I. Lana, *Due capitoli Prudeniziani* (Rome 1962); C. Gnilka, *Studien zur Psychomachie des Prudentius* (Wiesbaden 1963); K. Thraede, *Studien zur Sprache und Stil des Prudentius* (Göttingen 1965); R. Herzog, *Die allegorische Dicht-*

BIBLIOGRAPHY

TEXT AND COMMENTARY: TEXT: F. Vollmer (Berlin 1905). COMMENTARY: F. M. Clover (Philadelphia 1971: with tr. and reprint of Vollmer's text).

# SIDONIUS, GAIUS SOLLIUS APOLLINARIS

## LIFE

b. in Lyons *c*. A.D. 431, of distinguished family. Delivered verse panegyrics to emperors Avitus (whose daughter he had married 451), Majorian and Anthemius (*Carm*. 7, 5 and 2); appointed *Praefectus urbi* by the latter 468. Consecrated bishop of Auvergne 471 and organized resistance to the Visigoths. Briefly imprisoned by Euric 475, then resumed his bishopric and d. 486. Sources: Sidonius, *Epist*. 1.5, 1.8, 4.25, *Carm*. 13.23 (birthplace); *Epist*. 5.16, 3.12, 5.9, 8.6 (family); *Epist*. 5.16 (marriage); *Epist*. 4.12, 5.11 (children); *Carm*. 8.8, 9.16 (statue in forum); *Epist*. 1.9 (Praefectus); *Epist*. 3.1, 6.1 (bishop); *Epist*. 8.9, 9.3 (prisoner of Euric); *Epist*. 5.9, 8.6, 9.16 (old age); Gennadius, *De vir ill*. 92.

## WORKS

*Carmina*: twenty-four poems, including panegyrics, epithalamia and epistles, in various metres; pubd 469. *Epistulae*: nine books of letters dating from 455–60 to 482; dedicated to Constantius, priest of Lyons (*Epist*. 1.1, 7.18).

## BIBLIOGRAPHY

TEXTS: C. Luetjohann (Berlin 1887); P. Mohr (BT, 1895); W. B. Anderson (Loeb, 1936–65); A. Loyen (Budé, 1960–70).

STUDIES: C. E. Stevens, *Sidonius Apollinaris and his age* (Oxford 1933); H. Rutherford, *Sidonius Apollinaris. Études d'une figure gallo-romaine du Ve siècle* (Clermont-Ferrand 1938); A. Loyen, *Recherches historiques sur les Panégyriques de Sidoine Apollinaire* (Paris 1942); idem, *Sidoine Apollinaire et l'esprit précieux en Gaule aux derniers jours de l'empire* (Paris 1943); idem, 'Sidoine Apollinaire et les derniers éclats de la culture classique dans la Gaule occupée par les Goths', *Settimane di studio del Centro Italiano di studi sull'alto Medioevo* 3 (1955) 265–84; K. F. Stroheker, *Der senatorische Adel im spätantiken Gallien* (Tübingen 1948); N. K. Chadwick, *Poetry and letters in early Christian Gaul* (Cambridge 1955) 296–327; P. Courcelle, *Histoire littéraire des grandes invasions germaniques*, 3rd ed. (Paris 1964) 166–80, 235–9; idem, *Late Latin writers and their Greek sources* (Harvard 1969) 251–62.

# PAULINUS OF PELLA

## LIFE

b. A.D. 376 at Pella in Macedonia. Grandson of Ausonius and educated by him in Bordeaux. After Gothic invasions of Bordeaux and Bazas, compromised with the Alans and held office under Attalus in 410. Lived near Marseilles for many years, and later returned to Bordeaux. Sources: *Eucharisticon, passim*.

## BIBLIOGRAPHY

TEXTS: W. Brandes (Vienna 1888); H. G. Evelyn White, *Ausonius*, vol. II (Loeb, 1919); C. Moussy (Paris 1974); P. Courcelle, 'Un nouveau poème de Paulin de Pella', *V. Chr.* I (1947) 101–13.

TRANSLATION: J. Lindsay, *Song of a falling world* (London 1948) 190–9.

# HISTORIA AUGUSTA

Collection of lives of emperors and pretenders from Hadrian to Numerian; lives of Nerva and Trajan probably lost. Addressed to Diocletian, Constantine and other contemporaries, and purportedly written from before 305 till after 324. Attributed to six otherwise unknown authors. On date and purpose see excursus below. Sources: *Avid. Cass.* 3.3, *Marcus Aurelius* 19.21, *L. Verus* 11.4, *Macrinus* 15.4, *Aelius* 1.1, *Severus* 20.4, *Pescennius Niger* 9.1 (dedications to Diocletian); *Geta* 1.1, *Heliogabalus* 2.4, *Alexander Severus* 65.1, *Claudius* 4.2, *Maximinus* 1.1, *Gordiani* 34.6 (dedications to Constantine); *Proculus* 12.6, *Saturninus* 11.4, *Aurelian* 10.1 (methods); *Capitolinus et Balbinus* 4.5, *Triginta tyranni* 11.6 (aims); *Avidius Cassius* 9.5, *Hadrian* 12.4, *Pertinax* 15.8 (Marius Maximus); *Clodius* 12.14 (Herodian); *Alexander Severus* 49.3, *Gordiani* 2.1 (Dexippus).

# EXCURSUS ON THE NATURE AND DATE OF THE HISTORIA AUGUSTA

A certain disquiet regarding the obvious errors and inconsistencies of the *Hist. Aug.* was general in nineteenth-century scholarship, but there was no systematic attempt either to diagnose the peculiar features of these texts or to put forward a hypothesis to explain them. It was as a result of his work as editor of volume II of the *Prosopographia Imperii Romani* that Dessau in 1889 published a paper in which he mustered and analysed these errors and inconsistencies, and concluded that the work was a forgery, written by a single hand in the reign of Theodosius, drawing partly on the historical epitomes of Aurelius Victor and Eutropius, and containing veiled references to persons and events of the late fourth century.[1] The authors to whom the lives were attributed were creatures of the author's imagination. Historians who perforce made use of the *Hist. Aug.* were disconcerted to find the branch upon which they were sitting suddenly sawn off, and tried to save their sources from Dessau's destructive critique. This they could only do by supposing that texts of the Diocletianic or Constantinian periods had been worked over or edited by a later writer or writers. This was the view of Mommsen, who postulated a single editor in the Theodosian age.[2] The problem now became one of distinguishing original text and interpolations, a type of problem with which Mommsen's study of Roman law had made him familiar. Other scholars put forward similar hypotheses, sometimes involving more than one editor or reviser. This approach to the problem was pushed to its limit by von Domaszewski,[3] who postulated a series of editors who worked over the original text between the fourth and sixth centuries, 'bringing it up to date', rather as a standard legal text-book or Mrs Beeton's Cookery Book is regularly revised and re-edited. The difficulty, however, is to see why anyone should have wanted to revise such a collection of imperial biographies once, let alone many times over the course of two centuries. Von Domaszewski's position was almost a *reductio ad absurdum* of the whole concept of an original text subsequently revised. For a time some scholars, of whom the most distinguished was Baynes, argued that the *Hist. Aug.* was indeed a forgery, but that it should be dated in 360–2, when it was allegedly written as propaganda for the emperor Julian.[4] This theory has now been generally abandoned. The alleged allusions to items of Julian's policy are not at all clear. Recently Momigliano[5] has re-examined the whole problem and come to the tentative conclusion that Dessau's original charges are not proven, and that the *Hist. Aug.* may be just what it purports to be. His very cautious fundamentalist position has not inspired much enthusiasm, and most scholars today adhere to some variant of Dessau's hypothesis. Among these may be numbered Hartke,[6] Chastagnol,[7] Straub,[8] and Mazzarino.[9] All these seek some public or political motivation for the forgery. Syme[10] has recently argued with great cogency that the work may rather be inspired by the delight in mystification and invention for its own sake, a theory which would bring the *Hist. Aug.* closer to such romantic works of history as the pseudonymous accounts of the Trojan war or the Alexander Romance. The controversy continues.[11]

[1] H. Dessau, 'Über Zeit und Persönlichkeit der Scriptores Historiae Augustae', *Hermes* 24 (1889) 337–92.

[2] T. Mommsen, *Gesammelte Schriften* VII (Berlin 1909) 302–62.

[3] A. von Domaszewski, *S.H.A.W.* 7 (1916) 7, 15; 8 (1917) 1; 9 (1918) 6; 11 (1920) 6.

[4] N. H. Baynes, *The Historia Augusta. Its date and purpose* (Oxford 1926).

[5] A. Momigliano, 'An unsolved problem of historical forgery', *Journal of the Warburg and Courtauld Institutes* 17 (1954) 22–46 = *Studies in historiography* (London 1966) 143–80.

[6] W. Hartke, *Römische Kinderkaiser* (Berlin 1951).

[7] A. Chastagnol, *Recherches sur l'Histoire Auguste* (Bonn 1970).

[8] J. Straub, *Heidnische Geschichtsapologetik in der christlichen Spätantike* (Bonn 1963).

[9] S. Mazzarino, *Il pensiero storico classico* II (Bari 1966) 2 216–47.

[10] R. Syme, *Emperors and biography. Studies in the Historia Augusta* (Oxford 1971).

[11] Most recent survey of the literature by K. P. Johne, *Kaiser-biographie und Senatsaristokratie* (Berlin 1976) 11–46.

BIBLIOGRAPHY

TEXT: E. Hohl, suppl. C. Seyfarth and I. Samberger (BT, 1965).

STUDIES: Works cited in the footnotes to the excursus and the following: W. Hartke, *Geschichte und Politik im spätantiken Rom. Untersuchungen über die Scriptores Historiae Augustae* (Leipzig 1940); H. Stern, *Date et destinataire de l'Histoire Auguste* (Paris 1953); *Bonner Historia-Augusta Colloquium* 1–4 (1964–70); E. K. Merten, *Zwei Herrscherfeste in der Historia Augusta* (Bonn 1968); R. Syme, *Ammianus and the Historia Augusta* (Oxford 1968); F. Kolb, *Literarische Beziehungen zwischen Cassius Dio, Herodian und der Historia Augusta* (Bonn 1972); K. P. Johne, *Kaiserbiographie und Senatsaristokratie* (Berlin 1976: good summary of history of the problem 11–46); T. D. Barnes, *The sources of the Historia Augusta* (Brussels 1978).

## LATIN ALEXANDER ROMANCE

TEXTS: B. Kübler, *Iuli Valeri Alexandri Polemi Res Gestae Alexandri Macedonis* (Leipzig 1888); C. Müller, *Itinerarium Alexandri*, in F. Dübner, *Arriani opera* (Paris 1846); F. Pfister, *Der Alexanderroman des Archipresbyters Leo* (Heidelberg 1913).

## DICTYS CRETENSIS

Origin and date of work: Dictys, *Epistula*.
TEXT: W. Eisenhut (BT, 1958).

## DARES PHRYGIUS

TEXT: J. Meister (BT, 1873).

## AUGUSTINUS, AURELIUS (see also pp. 132–3)

### WORKS

*Confessions*: thirteen books, written *c.* A.D. 397. See August. *Retract.* 2.32, *Epist.* 231.6.

BIBLIOGRAPHY

TEXT: M. Skutella, 2nd ed. by H. Juergens and W. Schaub (Stuttgart 1969).

TRANSLATION: F. J. Sheed (London–New York 1943).

STUDIES: E. R. Dodds, 'Augustine's Confessions: a study of spiritual maladjustment', *Hibbert Journal* 26 (1927–8) 459–73; P. Courcelle, *Recherches sur les Confessions de S. Augustin* (Paris 1950); idem, *Les Confessions de S. Augustin dans la tradition littéraire: antécédents et postérité* (Paris 1963); C. Mohrmann, 'S. Augustin écrivain', *Recherches augustiniennes* 1 (1958) 43–66; H.-I. Marrou, *S. Augustin et la fin de la culture antique*, 4th ed. (Paris 1958); M. Pellegrino, *Les Confessions de S. Augustin* (Paris 1960); R. J. O'Connell, 'The riddle of Augustine's Confessions: a Plotinian key', *International Philosophical Quarterly* 4 (1964) 327–72; P. L. R. Brown, *Augustine of Hippo* (Oxford 1967) 158–81.

## IULIUS OBSEQUENS

TEXT: O. Rossbach, *T. Livi Periochae* (BT, 1910).

## IUSTINUS, MARCUS IUNIANUS

Author (possibly 3rd c. A.D.) of an epitome of Pompeius Trogus' *Historiae Philippicae*; see *praef.*

TEXT: O. Seel (BT, 1972); idem, *Pompei Trogi fragmenta* (BT, 1956).

STUDIES: L. Castiglione, *Studi intorno alle Storie Filippiche di Giustino* (Naples 1925); O. Seel, *Die Praefatio des Pompeius Trogus* (Erlangen 1955).

## ENMANN'S KAISERGESCHICHTE

STUDIES: H. Enmann, 'Eine verlorene Geschichte der römischen Kaiser und das Buch De viris illustribus urbis Romae', *Philologus* suppl. 4 (1884) 337–501; R. Syme, *Ammianus and the Historia Augusta* (Oxford 1968) 106ff.; idem, *Emperors and biography* (Oxford 1971) *passim*; W. den Boer, *Some minor Roman historians* (Leiden 1972) 21.

## AURELIUS VICTOR, SEXTUS;
## ORIGO GENTIS ROMANAE; DE VIRIS ILLUSTRIBUS

### LIFE OF AURELIUS

b. in Africa, probably *c.* A.D. 330. Rose from humble background to be appointed governor of Pannonia Secunda by Julian 361, and *Praefectus urbi* by Theodosius 389. Later details unknown. Sources: Amm. Marc. 21.10.6; Aur. Vict. *Caesares* 20.5; *CIL* VI 1186. Cf. *PLRE* I 960.

### WORKS

*Caesares*: résumé of Roman history from Augustus to Constantine II, written 360; see Jerome, *Epist.* 10.3; Lyd. *De Mag.* 3.7. Later combined with *Origo gentis Romanae* (covering legendary period) and *De viris illustribus* (biographies of regal and republican figures), both of unknown date and authorship.

### BIBLIOGRAPHY

TEXTS: F. Pichlmayr, corr. R. Gruendel (BT, 1966: includes *Origo* and *De vir. ill.*); P. Dufraigne (Budé, 1975). *De vir. ill.*: W. K. Sherwin (Norman, Oklahoma 1973: with tr.).

TRANSLATION: E. C. Echols, *Brief imperial lives* (Exeter 1962).

STUDIES: C. G. Starr, 'Aurelius Victor, historian of Empire', *Am. Hist. Rev.* 61 (1955/6) 574–86; E. Hohl, 'Die Historia Augusta und die Caesares des Aurelius Victor', *Historia* 4 (1955) 220–8; S. d'Elia, 'Per una nuova edizione critica di Aurelio Vittore', *Rendiconti dell'Accademia di Archeologia, Lettere e Belle Arti di Napoli* 43 (1968) 103–94; W. den Boer, *Some minor Roman historians* (Leiden 1972) 19–113. *Origo*: A. D. Momigliano, 'Some observations on the Origo gentis Romanae', *J.R.S,* 48 (1958) 56–73; idem, 'Per una nuova edizione dell'Origo gentis Romanae', *Athenaeum* 36 (1958) 248–59; G. Puccioni, 'Tradizione e innovazione nel linguaggio dell'Origo gentis Romanae', *S.I.F.C.* 30 (1958) 207–54. *De.vir. ill.*: L. Braccesi, *Introduzione al De viris illustribus* (Bologna 1973).

## EUTROPIUS

### LIFE

Accompanied Julian on Persian campaign A.D. 363 and was private secretary to Valens. Probably identical with E. who was proconsul of Asia 371–372, Praetorian Prefect of Illyricum 380–381, and consul 387. Sources: Nicephorus Gregoras, *Or. in Const. Magn.* in Lambecius, *Comm. de bibl. Vindob.* 8.136; *Scriptores Orig. Constantinopolitanae* 2.144; Amm. Marc. 29.1.36; Symm. *Epist.* 3.46–51; *Cod. Iust.* 1.54.4ᵃ etc.; *ILS* 5911. Cf. *PLRE* I 317.

### WORKS

*Breviarium ab urbe condita* (10 bks): survey of Roman history from foundation of city to accession of Valens 364; see Eutrop. *Brev. praef.*; Suda s.v. Εὐτρόπιος.

### BIBLIOGRAPHY

TEXT: H. Droysen (Berlin 1879); C. Santini (BT, 1979).

STUDIES: E. Malcovati, 'I breviari del quarto secolo', *Ann. Fac. Lettere e Filosofia Univ. Cagliari* 1 (1942) 23–65; W. den Boer, *Some minor Roman historians* (Leiden

1972) 114–72. *Greek translations*: Text in Droysen above. L. Baffetti, 'Di Peanio traduttore di Eutropio', *Byẕ. neugr. Jahrb.* 3 (1922) 15–36.

# FESTUS

## LIFE

b. Tridentum in Raetia. Governor of Syria late A.D. 360s, private secretary to Valens, and proconsul of Asia *c.* 372. Dismissed after Valens' death 378 and d. at Ephesus 380. Sources: Amm. Marc. 29.2.22–5; Liban. *Or.* 1.156–9; Eunap. *V.S.* 7.6.11–13. Cf. *PLRE* I 334–5.

## WORKS

*Breviarium rerum gestarum populi Romani*: compendium of Roman history from foundation of city to reign of Valens, written 369; see Fest. *Brev.* 1, 2, 10.

### BIBLIOGRAPHY

TEXT AND COMMENTARY: TEXT: C. Wagener (BT, 1886). COMMENTARY: J. W. Eadie (London 1967).

STUDIES: E. Malcovati, 'I breviari del quarto secolo', *Ann. Fac. Lettere e Filosofia Univ. Cagliari* I (1942) 23–65; W. den Boer, *Some minor Roman historians* (Leiden 1972) 173–223; B. Baldwin, 'Festus the historian', *Historia* 27 (1978) 192–217.

# EPITOME DE CAESARIBUS

TEXT: In F. Pichlmayr, *Sextus Aurelius De Caesaribus*, corr. R. Gruendel (BT,1966).

STUDIES: J. Schlumberger, *Die Epitome de Caesaribus. Untersuchungen ẕur heidnischen Geschichtsschreibung des 4. Jahrhunderts n. Chr.* (Munich 1974); W. Hartke, *Römische Kinderkaiser. Eine Strukturanalyse römischen Denkens und Daseins* (Berlin 1951) 375ff.

# EXCERPTUM VALESIANUM

TEXT: J. Moreau, rev. V. Velkov (BT, 1968).

# AMMIANUS MARCELLINUS

## LIFE

b. of Greek parents at Antioch *c.* A.D. 325–330. Served in the East and in Gaul under Ursicinus for seven years from 353/354, and joined Julian in his Persian campaign 363.

Visited Egypt, Greece (366) and Antioch (371), and later settled in Rome. Date of death unknown. Sources: Amm. Marc. *passim*, esp. 19.8.6, 14.9.1, 14.115, 15.5.22, 16.2.8, 16.10.21, 17.4.6, 18.8.11, 19.8.12, 21.5.7, 22.15.1., 24.1.5, 24.2.1, 24.5.1, 24.8.4, 25.1.1, 25.2.1, 25.3.1, 29.1.24, 29.2.16, 30.4.4; Liban. *Epist.* 983 (recitals of parts of his history at Rome). Cf. *PLRE* I 547–8.

## WORKS

*Res gestae*: continuation of Tacitus, originally in thirty-one books (A.D. 96–378), of which only 14–31 survive (starting in 353); written from 360s until possibly 395; see Amm. Marc. 31.16.9, 15.1.1, 16.1.3, 15.9.2, 28.1.2, 26.1.1, 27.2.11; Liban. *Epist.* 983.

## BIBLIOGRAPHY

TEXTS AND COMMENTARIES: TEXTS: C. U. Clark (Berlin 1910–15); J. C. Rolfe (Loeb, 1935–40); A. Selem (Turin 1965); W. Seyfarth (Berlin 1968–71); E. Galletier, J. Fontaine, G. Sabbah (Budé, 1968–). COMMENTARIES: P. de Jonge (Groningen 1935–); J. Szidat, *Historischer Kommentar zu Ammianus Marcellinus Buch* XX–XXI (Wiesbaden 1977–).

STUDIES: (1) GENERAL: W. Ensslin, *Zur Geschichtsschreibung und Weltanschauung des Ammianus Marcellinus* (Leipzig 1923); E. A. Thompson, *The historical work of Ammianus Marcellinus* (Cambridge 1947); C. P. T. Naudé, *Ammianus Marcellinus in die lig van die antieke geskiedskrywing* (Leiden 1956); S. Jannaccone, *Ammiano Marcellino* (Naples 1960); A. Demandt, *Zeitkritik und Geschichtsbild im Werk Ammians* (Bonn 1965); P. M. Camus, *Ammien Marcellin. Témoin des courants culturels et religieuses à la fin du IVe siècle* (Paris 1967); A. Momigliano, 'The lonely historian Ammianus Marcellinus', *A.S.N.P.* 4 (1974) 1393–1407; Z. V. Udal'tsova, *Idejno-politicheskaya bor'ba v rannej Vizantii* (Moscow 1974) 7–82; F. C. Blockley, *Ammianus Marcellinus. A study of his historiography and political thought* (Brussels 1975: with bibliography); J. M. Alonso-Nuñez, *La visión historiográfica de Ammiano Marcellino* (Valladolid 1975: with bibliography). (2) PARTICULAR TOPICS: G. B. Pighi, *I discorsi nelle storie di Ammiano Marcellino* (Milan 1936); A. Cameron, 'The Roman friends of Ammianus Marcellinus', *J.R.S.* 54 (1964) 15–28; F. Paschoud, *Roma aeterna. Études sur le patriotisme romain dans l'occident latin à l'époque des grandes invasions* (Rome 1967) 33–70; R. Syme, *Ammianus and the Historia Augusta* (Oxford 1968); C. Samberg, 'Die "Kaiserbiographie" in den Res Gestae des Ammianus Marcellinus', *Klio* 51 (1969) 349–482; H. Drexler, *Ammianstudien* (Hildesheim 1974); G. A. Crump, *Ammianus Marcellinus as a military historian* (Wiesbaden 1975).

# JEROME (HIERONYMUS)

## WORKS

*Chronicle*: survey of world history, an expanded translation (A.D. 380) from Eusebius of Caesarea; see *praef.* and *ann. Abr.* 2342. *De viris illustribus*: 135 notes on Christian writers from Peter to J. himself, written 392; see *praef.*

## BIBLIOGRAPHY

TEXTS: *Chron.* A. Schoene (Berlin 1866–75). *De vir. ill.* E. C. Richardson (BT, 1896); C. A. Bernoulli (Freiburg i. Br.–Leipzig 1895).

STUDIES: R. Helm, *Hieronymus' Zusätze in Eusebius' Chronik und ihre Wert für die Literaturgeschichte, Philologus* suppl. 21 (1929).

# RUFINUS

## WORKS

*Ecclesiastical history*: abbreviated translation from Eusebius of Caesarea, supplemented by two books covering 324–95; written A.D. 410s. See Gennadius, *De vir. ill.* 17.

TEXT: T. Mommsen, in E. Schwartz, *Eusebius' Kirchengeschichte* (BT, 1903) vol. II.

# SULPICIUS SEVERUS

## WORKS

*Chronicle* (2 bks): Christian history from creation to A.D. 400; see Gennadius, *De vir. ill.* 19, Sulp. Sev. *Chron.* 1.1.

## BIBLIOGRAPHY

TEXTS: C. Halm (Vienna 1866); A. Lavertujon (Paris 1896–9).

STUDIES: N. K. Chadwick, *Poetry and letters in early Christian Gaul* (Cambridge 1955) 89–121.

# AUGUSTINUS, AURELIUS (see also pp. 127–8)

*De civitate dei* (22 bks): vindication of the Christian church, pubd A.D. 413–425; see *Retract.* 2.43.1.

BIBLIOGRAPHY

TEXTS: B. Dombart and A. Kalb (BT, 1928–9); G. E. McCracken (London 1957–72).

STUDIES: H.-I. Marrou, *S. Augustin et la fin de la culture antique*, 2nd ed. (Paris 1949); R. H. Barrow, *Introduction to St. Augustine*, '*The City of God*' (London 1950); J. Straub, 'Augustins Sorge um die regeneratio imperii. Das imperium als civitas terrena', *H.J.* 73 (1954) 36–60; F. G. Maier, *Augustin und das antike Rom* (Stuttgart 1955); P. L. R. Brown, *Augustine of Hippo* (London 1967) 299–329; F. Paschoud, *Roma aeterna. Études sur le patriotisme romain dans l'occident latin à l'époque des grandes invasions* (Rome 1967) 234–75.

# OROSIUS

## LIFE

b. in Spain *c.* A.D. 375–380. Went to Augustine in Hippo *c.* 410–412 and returned there after visiting Jerome in Bethlehem 415. Date of death unknown. Sources: Gennadius, *De vir. ill.* 39; Oros. *Hist.* 7.22.8; August. *Epist.* 166.2, 169.13; Braulio Caesaraugustensis, *Epist.* 44 (Migne, *PL* LXXX 698D); Avitus presbyter, *Ep. ad Balchonium* (Migne, *PL* XLI 806).

## WORKS

*Historiarum adversus paganos libri VII*: anti-pagan Roman history, completed 417/418; see Hist. 1 *prol.* 1ff.; 7.43.19.

TEXT: C. Zangemeister (Vienna 1882).

TRANSLATION: I. W. Raymond (New York 1936).

STUDIES: J. Svennung, *Orosiana* (Uppsala 1922); G. Fink-Errara, 'San Augustin y Orosio', *Ciudad de Dios* 167 (1954) 455–549; B. Lacroix, *Orose et ses idées* (Paris 1965: with bibliography).

# LATIN RHETORICIANS

TEXT: C. Halm, *Rhetores Latini minores* (BT, 1863).

STUDIES: M. L. Clarke, *Rhetoric at Rome*, 2nd ed. (London 1966); G. Kennedy, *The art of rhetoric in the Roman world* (Princeton 1972).

# PANEGYRICI LATINI

## LIVES

Latinius Pacatus Drepanius: *Pan. Lat.* 12.1.3 etc.; Sid. Apoll. *Epist.* 8.11; Auson. pp. 86, 155, 169 Peiper; *Cod. Theod.* 10.2.4ª, 9.42.13ª. Cf. *PLRE* I 272.

Claudius Mamertinus: *ILS* 755; Amm. Marc. 21.8.1, 21.10.8, 21.12.25, 22.31, 26.55, 27.7.1. Cf. *PLRE* I 540–1.

Nazarius: Jerome, *Chron.* A.D. 324, 336; Auson. *Prof. Burd.* 15.7–10. Cf. *PLRE* I 618–19.

Eumenius: *Pan. Lat.* 5.1.1, 5.11.2, 5.14.1–3, 5.17.3–4. Cf. *PLRE* I 294–5.

## BIBLIOGRAPHY

TEXTS: E. Galletier (Budé, 1949–55); R. A. B. Mynors (OCT, 1964); W. J. G. Lubbe, *Incerti panegyricus Constantino Augusto dictus* (Leiden 1955); H. Gutzwiller, *Die Neujahrsrede des Konsuls Claudius Mamertinus vor dem Kaiser Julian* (Basel 1942); G. Barabino, *Claudio Mamertino. Il panegirico dell'Imperatore Giuliano* (Genoa 1965).

STUDIES: W. S. Maguinness, 'Some methods of the Latin panegyrists', *Hermathena* 47 (1932) 42–61; idem, 'Locutions and formulae of the Latin panegyrists', *Hermathena* 48 (1933) 117–38; E. Vereecke, 'Le corpus des panégyriques latins de l'époque tardive. Problèmes d'imitation', *A.C.* 44 (1975) 141–60.

# SYMMACHUS, QUINTUS AURELIUS

## LIFE

b. *c.* A.D. 345 of distinguished Roman family; studied rhetoric under tutor from Bordeaux. Governor of Bruttium 365, Proconsul of Africa 373–374, *Praefectus urbi* 384–385, consul 391. d. after 402. Sources: full refs. in *PLRE* I 865–70.

## WORKS

Eight speeches, including two panegyrics addressed to Valentinian (369 and 370) and one to Gratian (369), and ten books of letters, written between 364 and 402 and pubd after his death; bk 10 (*Relationes*) comprises official reports sent by S. as *Praefectus urbi* to Valentinian II. See Socr. *Hist eccl.* 5.14; Symm. *Epist.* tit., 3.11, 5.85, 5.86; Macrob. 5.1.7; Prudent. *c. Symm.* 1.632; Sid. Apoll. *Epist.* 1.1.

## BIBLIOGRAPHY

TEXTS: O. Seeck (Berlin 1883). *Letters*: J. P. Callu (Budé, 1972). *Relationes*: R. H. Barrow (Oxford 1973).

STUDIES: S. Dill, *Roman society in the last century of the western empire*, 2nd ed. (London 1910) 143–66; J. A. MacGeachy, *Q. Aurelius Symmachus and the senatorial aristocracy of the west* (Chicago 1947); D. Romano, *Simmaco* (Palermo 1955); F. Paschoud, *Roma aeterna. Études sur le patriotisme romain dans l'occident latin à l'époque des grandes invasions* (Rome 1967) 71–109; F. Canfora, *Simmaco e Ambrogio* (Bari 1970); R. Klein, *Symmachus* (Darmstadt 1971); idem, *Der Streit um den Victoria-Altar* (Darmstadt 1972); J. F. Matthews, 'The letters of Symmachus', in (ed.) J. W. Binns, *Latin literature of the fourth century* (London 1974) 58–99; idem, *Western aristocracies and imperial court AD 364–425* (Oxford 1975).

# MACROBIUS AMBROSIUS THEODOSIUS

## WORKS

*Commentary on the dream of Scipio*: discussion of dream recounted in Cic. *Rep.*; see *Comm.* 1.5.1. *Saturnalia* (7 bks; parts missing): purported account of symposium held during Saturnalia of 384; see *praef.*, 1.15. *De differentiis et societatibus graeci latinique verbi*: fragments in *GLK* v 599ff.

## BIBLIOGRAPHY

TEXT: J. Willis (BT, 1963).

TRANSLATION: *Comm.*: W. H. Stahl (New York 1952).

STUDIES: T. Whittaker, *Philosophy, science and letters in the year 400* (Cambridge 1923); K. Mras, 'Macrobius' Kommentar zu Ciceros Somnium, ein Beitrag zur Geistesgeschichte des V. Jahrh. n.Chr.', *S.P.A.W.* 1933, 6.232–86; A. Cameron, 'The date and identity of Macrobius', *J.R.S.* 56 (1966) 25–38; P. Courcelle, *Late Latin writers and their Greek sources* (Cambridge, Mass. 1969) 13–47; J. Flamant, *Macrobe et le Néo-Platonisme latin à la fin du IVe siècle* (Leiden 1977).

# MARTIANUS MIN(N)E(I)US FELIX CAPELLA

## LIFE

Lived in Carthage, possibly a teacher of rhetoric; see *Nupt. Phil. et Merc.* 9.997, 6.577.

## WORKS

*De nuptiis Philologiae et Mercurii* (9 bks): prose and verse encyclopaedia of the liberal arts, which are introduced allegorically as handmaids to Philologia at her marriage to Mercury, god of eloquence; see 1.3, 1.5.

BIBLIOGRAPHY

TEXT AND COMMENTARY: TEXT: A. Dick (BT, 1925). COMMENTARY: Bk 2: L. Lenaz (Padua 1975).

TRANSLATION: W. H. Stahl, R. Johnson, E. L. Burge (Columbia 1977).

STUDIES: H. W. Fischer, *Untersuchungen über die Quellen der Rhetorik des Martianus Capella* (Breslau 1936); G. Leonardi, *I codici di Marziano Capella* (Milan 1960); P. Courcelle, *Late Latin writers and their Greek sources* (Cambridge, Mass. 1969) 211– 19; W. H. Stahl, *Martianus Capella and the seven liberal arts* (New York – London 1971).

## SACERDOS, MARIUS PLOTIUS

TEXT: *GLK* VI 415–546.

## CHARISIUS, FLAVIUS SOSIPATER

TEXT: *GLK* I 1–296; C. Barwick (BT, 1925).

## DIOMEDES

TEXT: *GLK* I 298–592.

## DONATUS, AELIUS

### LIFE

*fl.* A.D. 353; teacher of Jerome.

### WORKS

*Ars grammatica* in two versions (*Ars minor* and *Ars maior*), and commentaries on Virgil (introduction survives) and Terence (extant version probably modified). Sources: Jerome, *Chron.* A.D. 353; *Comm. in Eccles.* 1; *Apol. adv. Rufin.* 1.16; *Prisc. GLK* III 281, 320 etc.

TEXT: *GLK* IV 355–402. *Comm. Ter.*: P. Wessner (BT, 1902–8).

# MARIUS VICTORINUS AFER, GAIUS

## LIFE

*fl.* mid-4th *c.* A.D. Jerome's teacher of rhetoric and intellectual leader of Roman Neoplatonists. Converted to Christianity in old age. Sources: Jerome, *De vir. ill.* 101, *Comm. in Galat. praef.*, *Chron.* A.D. 353.

## WORKS

(Partly extant). *Ars grammatica*, four books on metre; translations of Greek philosophers; commentaries on Aristotle and Cicero's *De inventione* and *Topica*; Christian treatises, commentaries and poems. See August. *Conf.* 8.2; Cassiod. *Inst.* 2, *Rhet.* 10 (Halm p. 153); *PLRE* I 964.

## BIBLIOGRAPHY

TEXTS: *GLK* VI 1–184; C. Helm, *Rhetores Latini minores* 153–304; T. Stangl, *Tulliana et Mario-Victoriana* (Munich 1888); Migne, *PL* VIII (Paris 1844); P. Hadot, *Marius Victorinus. Opera theologica* (Vienna 1971); P. Henry and P. Hadot, *Marius Victorinus. Traités théologiques sur la Trinité* (Paris 1960); A. Locher, *Marius Victorinus. Opera theologica* (BT, 1976).

STUDIES: P. Hadot, *Porphyre et Victorinus* (Paris 1968); H. Dahlmann, 'Zur Ars grammatica des Marius Victorinus', *Abh. Akad. Mainz* 1970, 2; P. Hadot, *Marius Victorinus. Recherches sur sa vie et ses oeuvres* (Paris 1971).

# SERVIUS

## LIFE

Unknown: his presence as a young man in Macrobius' *Saturnalia* (1.2.15, 6.6.1) is probably an anachronism.

## WORKS

Commentary on Virgil, probably written A.D. 420s, surviving also in a version supplemented by material from other commentators (Servius *auctus* or Servius Danielis). See Prisc. *GLK* II 256.14, 515.23 etc.

## BIBLIOGRAPHY

TEXTS: *GLK* IV 405–565; G. Thilo and H. Hagen (BT, 1889–1902); E. K. Rand et al., *Servianorum in Vergilii carmina commentariorum editionis Harvardianae*, vols. II–III (Lancaster, Pa. 1946–65).

STUDIES: J. F. Mountford and J. T. Schulz, *Index rerum et hominum in scholiis Servii et Aeli Donati tractatorum* (New York 1930); G. Funaioli, *Esegesi virgiliana antica* (Milan 1930); A. Cameron, 'The date and identity of Macrobius', *J.R.S.* 56 (1966) 25–38; G. P. Goold, 'Servius and the Helen episode', *H.S.Ph.* 74 (1970) 101–68; C. E. Murgia, *Prolegomena to Servius 5: the manuscripts* (Berkeley–Los Angeles–London 1975).

# DONATUS, TIBERIUS CLAUDIUS

## WORKS

*Interpretationes Vergilianae*: commentary on *Aeneid* in twelve books; see *praef.* and *PLRE* I 268–9.

TEXT: H. Georgii (BT, 1905–6).

# NONIUS MARCELLUS

## LIFE

African, probably active first half of 4th c. A.D.

## WORKS

*De compendiosa doctrina*: lexicon of Republican Latin in twenty books (bk 16 lost); see *subscriptio* to *De comp. doct.* and *CIL* VIII 4878.

## BIBLIOGRAPHY

TEXT: W. M. Lindsay (BT, 1903).

STUDIES: W. M. Lindsay, *Nonius Marcellus' dictionary of Republican Latin* (Oxford 1901); A. Coucke, *Nonius Marcellus en zijn De compendiosa doctrina* (Louvain 1936–7); F. Bertini and G. Barabino (edd.), *Studi Noniani* I–IV (Genoa 1967–77).

# MATERNUS, IULIUS FIRMICUS

## LIFE

Sicilian of senatorial rank; practised as advocate.

## WORKS

*Matheseos libri VIII*: handbook of astrology, written 330s or 340s. *De errore profanorum religionum*: anti-pagan polemic attributed in MSS to Julius Firmicus Maternus, and possibly written by the author of the preceding.

## BIBLIOGRAPHY

TEXTS AND COMMENTARY: TEXTS: *Math.*: W. Kroll, F. Skutsch, K. Ziegler (BT, 1897–1913). *De errore*: K. Ziegler (BT, 1908). COMMENTARY: *De errore*: C. Heuten (Leipzig 1908).

STUDIES: F. Boll, *Sphaera* (Leipzig 1903) 394ff.; F. H. Cramer, *Astrology in Roman law and politics* (Philadelphia 1954); T. Wilkström, *In Firmicum Maternum studia critica* (Uppsala 1935).

# PALLADIUS RUTILIUS TAURUS AEMILIANUS

## LIFE

4th c. A.D. Owner of estates in Italy and Sardinia (4.10.16 and 24).

## WORKS

*De re rustica* (15 bks), comprising an introductory book, one book for each month of the year, a book on the care of farm-animals (*De veterinaria medicina*; first pubd by Svennung, see below), and a book in elegiacs on the cultivation of trees (*De insitione*).

## BIBLIOGRAPHY

TEXTS: R. H. Rodgers (BT, 1975: with bibliography). *De vet. med.*: J. Svennung (Göteborg 1926: ed. princ.).

STUDIES: H. Widstrand, *Palladiusstudien* (Uppsala 1926); J. Svennung, 'De auctoribus Palladii', *Eranos* 25 (1927) 123–78, 230–48; idem, *Untersuchungen zu Palladius und zur lateinischen Fach- und Volkssprache* (Uppsala 1935); K. D. White, *Agricultural implements of the Roman world* (Cambridge 1967); idem, *Roman farming* (London 1970); idem, *Farm equipment of the Roman world* (Cambridge 1975); R. H. Rodgers, *An introduction to Palladius* (London 1975).

# VEGETIUS RENATUS, FLAVIUS

## WORKS

*Epitoma rei militaris*: four books on Roman military system, written between A.D. 383 (ref. to *divi Gratiani* 1.20) and 450 (revision made by Eutropius of Alexandria); dedicated to an emperor, probably Theodosius I. *Mulomedicina*: six books on veterinary science, attributed in MSS to P. Vegetius, probably identical with author of the *Epitoma*.

## BIBLIOGRAPHY

TEXTS: *Epitoma*: C. Lang, 2nd ed. (BT, 1885; repr. 1967). *Mulomedicina*: E. Lommatzsch (BT, 1903).

STUDIES: D. Schenk, *Flavius Vegetius Renatus. Die Quellen der Epitoma rei militaris* (Leipzig 1930); A. Andersson, *Studia Vegetiana* (Uppsala 1938); F. Rayniers, *Végèce et l'instruction des cadres et de la troupe dans l'armée romaine* (Nancy 1938).

# DE REBUS BELLICIS

TEXT AND COMMENTARY: E. A. Thompson, *A Roman reformer and inventor* (Oxford 1952).

# ARNOBIUS

## LIFE AND WORKS

b. *c*. A.D. 240; teacher of rhetoric and advocate from Sicca Veneria in Africa. After his conversion to Christianity in the early 4th c. wrote *Adversus nationes*, an attack on paganism in seven books. Sources: Jerome, *Chron.* A.D. 326 (possible year of death), *De vir. ill* 79, *Epist.* 58; Arnobius 1.1, 1.13, 2.71.

## BIBLIOGRAPHY

TEXT: C. Marchesi (Turin 1934).

STUDIES: W. Kroll, 'Arnobiusstudien', *Rh.M.* 72 (1917) 63–112; F. Gabarrou, *Arnobe, son oeuvre* (Paris 1921); idem, *Le latin d'Arnobe* (Paris 1921); H. Hagendahl, *La prose métrique d'Arnobe* (Göteborg 1936); E. Rapisarda, *Arnobio* (Catania 1946).

# APULEIUS

## LIFE

b. *c.* A.D. 125 at Madauros (August. *C.D.* 8.14; *Epist.* 102.32). Educ. Carthage (*Flor.* 18.15) and Athens (*Apol.* 72.3, *Flor.* 18.15); visited Rome (*Flor.* 17.4). Arrived Oea 155–156 and married Pudentilla (*Apol.* 73ff.). Indicted for magic at Sabrata 158–159 (on the date, R. Syme, *R.E.A.* 61 (1959) 316f.). Subsequent life at Carthage as chief priest (*Flor.* 16.38); honorific statues to him (*Flor.* 16.1ff.). No evidence after 170.

## WORKS

(1) EXTANT: *Apology* 158–159, *Florida c.* 160–170, *Metamorphoses*, date uncertain, probably after 160. Of the philosophical works (dates uncertain), *De deo Socratis* is undisputed, *De dogmate Platonis* and *De mundo* are probably A.'s, Περὶ ἑρμηνείας is possibly his, but *Asclepius* is spurious. (2) LOST: Love-lyrics and satirical poetry in Catullan mode (*Apol.* 6.3, 9.12ff.); hymns (*Flor.* 17.18, 18.37ff.); other poetry (*Flor.* 9.27f., 20.6); speeches (*Apol.* 55.10, August. *Epist.* 138.19); *Hermagoras*, a romance (Prisc. *GLK* II 85 and Fulg. p. 122 Helm); *Eroticus*, anthology of love-stories (Lydus, *Mag.* 3.64); *Epitome historiarum* (? = collection of abbreviated stories; Prisc. *GLK* III 482); *Quaestiones convivales* (Sid. Apoll. 9.13.3 and Macr. *Sat.* 7.3.23); *De republica* (Fulg. p. 122 Helm); translation of *Phaedo* (Sid. Apoll. 2.9.5); *Quaestiones naturales* (*Apol.* 36ff.); *De proverbiis* (Charisius, *GLK* I 240); *Arithmetica* (Cassiod. *Arithm.*); *De musica* (Cassiod. *Mus.*); *De re rustica* (Palladius 1.35.9); *De arboribus* (Serv. *ad* Virg. *G.* 2.126); *Medicinalia* (Prisc. *GLK* II 203).

## BIBLIOGRAPHY

(up to 1970, see Bursian 171 (1915) 147ff., 175 (1919) 1ff.; D. S. Robertson, *Y.W.C.S.* 1938, 94ff.; C. C. Schlam, *C.W.* 64 (1971) 285ff.)

TEXTS AND COMMENTARIES: TEXTS: Complete: R. Helm and P. Thomas, 1st–3rd edd. (BT, 1955–69). *Apol.* and *Flor.*: P. Vallette (Budé, 1960). *Philosophica*: J. Beaujeu (Budé, 1973: *De deo Socr.*, *De Platone*, *De mundo*). *Met.*: D. S. Robertson (Budé, 1940–5). COMMENTARIES: *Apol.*: H. E. Butler and A. S. Owen (Oxford 1914); B. Mosca (Florence 1974). *Met.*: Bk 1: A. Scobie (Meisenheim 1975). Bk 2: B. J. de Jonge (Groningen 1941). Bk 3: R. T. van der Paardt (Amsterdam 1971). Bk 4.1–27: B. L. Hijmans et al. (Groningen 1977). *Cupid and Psyche*: L. C. Purser (London 1910); P. Grimal (Paris 1963). Bk 11: J. G. Griffiths (Leiden 1975).

STUDIES: P. Junghanns, *Die Erzählungstechnik von Apuleius' Metamorphoses und ihrer Vorlage* (Leipzig 1932); M. Bernhard, *Der Stil des Apuleius von Madaura*, 2nd ed. (Amsterdam 1965); B. E. Perry, *The ancient romances* (Berkeley 1967); P. G. Walsh,

*The Roman novel* (Cambridge 1970); (edd.) B. L. Hijmans and R. T. van der Paardt, *Aspects of the Golden Ass* (Groningen 1978); J. Tatum, *Apuleius and the Golden Ass* (Ithaca 1979). See also recent bibliographies in edd. of Beaujeu, Scobie and Griffiths above.

## EPILOGUE

Bolgar, R. R., *The classical heritage and its beneficiaries* (Cambridge 1954).

idem (ed.), *Classical influences on European culture AD 500–1500* (Cambridge 1971).

de Ghellink, J., *Littérature latine au moyen age*, 2 vols. (Paris 1939).

idem, *L'essor de la littérature latine au XII* siècle* (Brussels 1955).

Hagendahl, H., *Latin fathers and the classics* (Göteborg 1958).

Highet, G., *The classical tradition* (London 1949).

Laistner, M. L. W., *Thought and letters in western Europe, AD 500–900* (London 1931).

Manitius, M., *Geschichte der lateinischen Literatur des Mittelalters*, 3 vols. (Munich 1911–31).

Raby, F. J. E., *A history of secular Latin poetry in the middle ages*, 2 vols., 2nd ed. (Oxford 1957).

idem, *A history of Christian-Latin poetry*, 2nd ed. (Oxford 1953).

# METRICAL APPENDIX

## (1) BASIC PRINCIPLES

### (A) STRESSED AND QUANTITATIVE VERSE

In metres familiar to speakers of English, rhythm is measured by the predictable alternation of one or more stressed syllables with one or more unstressed syllables (distinguished by the notation – and ◡, or ′ and ×). Consequently, it is word-accent that
determines whether or not a word or sequence of words may stand in a certain part of
the verse. Thus the word *classical* may occupy the metrical unit represented by the
notation –◡◡ by virtue of the stress imparted to its first syllable in everyday pro-
nunciation. In contrast, the rhythms of classical Latin metres are measured by the
predictable alternation of one or more 'heavy' syllables with one or more 'light'
syllables (defined below, and distinguished by the notation – and ◡), so that in the
construction of Latin verse the factor of primary importance is not word-accent but
syllabic 'weight'. Thus the word *facerent*, although accented in normal speech on the
first syllable, consists for metrical purposes of two light syllables followed by one
heavy syllable, and for this reason can only occupy the metrical unit ◡◡–. Verse constructed upon this principle is conventionally designated *quantitative*: it should be
emphasized that this term refers to the quantity (or 'weight') of syllables, and that
throughout this account such quantity is described by the terms 'heavy' and 'light' to
distinguish it from the intrinsic length of vowels; unfortunately, both syllabic weight
and vowel-length are still generally denoted by the same symbols, – and ◡.

### (B) SYLLABIFICATION

A syllable containing a long vowel or diphthong is heavy (e.g. the first syllables of
*pacem* and *laudo*).

A syllable containing a short vowel is light if it ends with that vowel (e.g. the first
syllable of *pecus*), but heavy if it ends with a consonant (e.g. the first syllable of *pectus*).

To decide whether or not a short-vowelled syllable ends with a consonant (and thus
to establish its quantity), the following rules should be observed:[1] (i) word-division

---

[1] The resulting division is practical only; for the difficulties involved in an absolute definition
of the syllabic unit see Allen (1973) under (4) below, esp. 27–40.

should be disregarded; (ii) a single consonant between two vowels or diphthongs belongs to the succeeding syllable (thus *pecus →pe–cus*; *genus omne →ge–nu–som–ne*); (iii) of two or more successive consonants, at least one belongs to the preceding syllable (thus *pectus →pec–tus*; also *nulla spes →nul–las–pes*, though short final vowels are normally avoided in this position), except as allowed for below.

*Note*: for this purpose *h* is disregarded; *x* and *ʒ* count as double consonants, 'semi-consonantal' *i* and *u* as consonants (except in the combination *qu*, regarded as a single consonant).

To (iii) there is an important exception. In the case of the combination of a plosive and liquid consonant (*p, t, c, b, d, g* followed by *r* or *l*), the syllabic division may be made either between the consonants (e.g. *pat–ris*) or before them (e.g. *pa–tris*), resulting in *either* a heavy *or* a light preceding syllable. However, when two such consonants belong to different parts of a compound or to two different words, the division is always made between them, giving a heavy preceding syllable (e.g. *ablego → ab–lego*, not *a–blego*; *at rabidae →at–rabidae*, not *a–trabidae*). Lastly, when, after a short final vowel, these consonants begin the next word, the division is nearly always made before them, giving a light preceding syllable (e.g. *plumbea glans →plum–be–a–glans*).

## (C) ACCENT

The nature of the Latin word-accent (whether one of pitch or stress) and its importance in the construction of verse are both matters of controversy: for a clear discussion of the basic problems see Wilkinson under (4) below, 89–96, 221–36. By way of practical guidance in reading Latin verse, all that may be said is that for the present-day English speaker, accustomed to a naturalistic manner of reading poetry, it will sound as strange (and monotonous) to emphasize the heavy syllables of a metrical structure ('Quális Théseá iacuít cedénte carína') as it does to read Shakespearian verse with attention only to its iambic structure ('Now ís the wínter óf our díscontént'); furthermore that, even in giving stress to the word-accent in Latin verse, heavy syllables will generally coincide with accented syllables with sufficient frequency to ensure that the metre is not forgotten – particularly at the beginning and end of many metres, as in the hexameter quoted above. It should be remembered, however, that what sounds natural is not thereby authentic, and that poetic delivery is highly susceptible to whims of fashion, idiosyncrasy and affectation. Even now it is not uncommon criticism of a Shakespearian actor that he 'mutilates' the shape of the verse by reading it as prose, while recordings of Tennyson and Eliot reading their poetry already sound bizarre (in different ways) to the modern ear.

## (2) TECHNICAL TERMS

*Anceps* ('unfixed'): term used to describe a metrical element which may be represented by either a heavy or a light syllable. The final element of many Latin metres is regularly of this nature, but not in certain lyric metres in which there is metrical continuity (*synaphea*) between as well as within lines.

*Brevis brevians*, or *the law of iambic shortening*: in comedy and other early Latin verse a heavy syllable may be lightened if it directly follows a light syllable and is adjacent to an accented syllable.

*Caesura* ('cutting') and *diaeresis*: division between words within a verse is termed *caesura* when occurring inside a metrical foot, or *diaeresis* when occurring at the end of a foot. The varied distribution of these plays an important part in avoiding monotony in the structure of verse; in particular, the caesura prevents a succession of words co-extensive with the feet of a metre (as found in Ennius' hexameter, 'sparsis hastis longis campus splendet et horret').

*Elision* and *hiatus*: a vowel (or vowel + *m*) ending a word is generally suppressed or *elided* when immediately preceding another vowel or *h*. When it is not elided in these circumstances (a phenomenon most frequently found in comedy), it is said to be in *hiatus*; by the rare process of *correption* a long vowel or diphthong in hiatus may be scanned short to make a light syllable. *Prodelision* (or *aphaeresis*) signifies the suppression of *e* in *est* after a final vowel or *m*, *hypermetric elision* the suppression of a vowel between lines (nearly always that of *–que*).

*Resolution*: the substitution of two light syllables for a heavy one.

## (3) COMMON METRES

For the sake of simplicity only the most basic characteristics of each metre are given here. For the numerous divergencies regarding anceps, resolution, position of caesura etc., see Raven under (4) below.

(a) Stichic verse (constructed by repetition of the same metrical line)
Iambic senarius (or trimeter):

$$\times-\cup-\,|\,\times-\cup-\,|\,\times-\cup\times$$

(commonest dialogue metre in early Roman drama; also used in Seneca's tragedies, Phaedrus' *Fables*, and, in alternation with an iambic dimeter ( $=\times-\cup-\,|\,\times-\cup-$ ), Horace's *Epodes* 1–10)
Iambic septenarius (or tetrameter catalectic):

$$\times-\cup-\,|\,\times-\cup-\,|\,\times-\cup-\,|\,\cup-\times$$

(common dialogue metre of comedy)

145

Trochaic septenarius (or tetrameter catalectic):

$$-\cup-\underline{\cup}\,|\,-\cup-\underline{\cup}\,|\,-\cup-\underline{\cup}\,|\,-\cup\underline{\cup}$$

(very common dialogue metre in early Roman drama)

Hexameter:

$$-\underline{\cup\cup}\,|\,-\underline{\cup\cup}\,|\,-\underline{\cup\cup}\,|\,-\underline{\cup\cup}\,|\,-\cup\cup\,|\,-\underline{\cup}$$

(regular metre for epic, satiric, pastoral and didactic poetry)

Pentameter:

$$-\underline{\cup\cup}-\underline{\cup\cup}-\,|\,-\cup\cup-\cup\cup\underline{\cup}$$

(following the hexameter this forms the elegiac couplet, which is regarded as an entity and hence as stichic; regular metre for love-poetry and epigram)

Phalaecean hendecasyllables:

$$\underline{\cup\overline{\cup}}\,|\,-\cup\cup-\,|\,\cup-\cup-\underline{\cup}$$

(i.e. first foot may be a spondee, iamb or trochee; used by Catullus, Martial and Statius)

(b) Non-stichic verse (constructed by combination of different metrical lines)

| | | |
|---|---|---|
| Alcaic stanza: | $--\cup--\,|\,-\cup\cup-\,|\,\cup\underline{\cup}$ | (twice) |
| | $--\cup---\cup\underline{\cup}$ | |
| | $-\cup\cup-\cup\cup-\,|\,\cup-\underline{\cup}$ | |
| Sapphic stanza: | $-\cup--\,|\,-\cup\cup-\,|\,\cup-\underline{\cup}$ | (three times) |
| | $-\cup\cup-\,|\,\underline{\cup}$ | (adonean) |
| Third asclepiad: | $--\,|\,-\cup\cup-\,|\,\cup\underline{\cup}$ | (glyconic) |
| | $--\,|\,-\cup\cup--\cup\cup-\,|\,\cup\underline{\cup}$ | (lesser asclepiad) |
| Fourth asclepiad: | $--\,|\,-\cup\cup--\cup\cup-\,|\,\cup\underline{\cup}$ | (lesser asclepiad, three times) |
| | $--\,|\,-\cup\cup-\,|\,\cup\underline{\cup}$ | (glyconic) |
| Fifth asclepiad | $--\,|\,-\cup\cup--\cup\cup-\,|\,\cup\underline{\cup}$ | (lesser asclepiad, twice) |
| | $--\,|\,-\cup\cup-\,|\,\underline{\cup}$ | (pherecratean) |
| | $--\,|\,-\cup\cup-\,|\,\cup\underline{\cup}$ | (glyconic) |

(the First and Second asclepiad consist, respectively, of the lesser and greater asclepiad only; the latter $=--\,|\,-\cup\cup--\cup\cup--\cup\cup-\,|\,\cup\underline{\cup}$)

All the above found in Horace's *Odes*; some in Catullus and Statius.


# (4) BIBLIOGRAPHY

Allen, W. S., *Vox Latina*, 2nd ed. (Cambridge 1978).

idem, *Accent and rhythm* (Cambridge 1973).

Raven, D. S., *Latin metre* (London 1965).

Wilkinson, L. P., *Golden Latin artistry* (Cambridge 1963) 89–134 and *passim*

# ABBREVIATIONS

| | |
|---|---|
| *Anth. Lat.* | A. Riese–F. Bücheler–E. Lommatzsch, *Anthologia Latina* *Latina* (Leipzig, 1894–1926). (Cf. *CLE*) |
| *ANRW* | H. Temporini, *Aufstieg und Niedergang der römischen Welt* (Berlin, 1972– ) |
| Bardon | H. Bardon, *La littérature latine inconnue* (Paris 1951–6) |
| BT | Bibliotheca Scriptorum Graecorum et Romanorum Teubneriana (Leipzig & Stuttgart) |
| Budé | Collection des Universités de France, publiée sous le patronage de l'Association Guillaume Budé (Paris) |
| Bursian | Bursian's *Jahresbericht über die Fortschritte der klassischen Altertumswissenschaft* (Berlin, 1873–1945) |
| *CAF* | T. Kock, *Comicorum Atticorum Fragmenta* (Leipzig, 1880–8) |
| *CAH* | *The Cambridge Ancient History* (Cambridge, 1923–39) |
| *CAH²* | 2nd ed. (Cambridge, 1961– ) |
| *CC* | *Corpus Christianorum.* Series Latina (Turnholt, 1953– ) |
| *CGF* | G. Kaibel, *Comicorum Graecorum Fragmenta* (Berlin, 1899) |
| *CGFPap.* | C. F. L. Austin, *Comicorum Graecorum Fragmenta in papyris reperta* (Berlin, 1973) |
| *CIL* | *Corpus Inscriptionum Latinarum* (Berlin, 1863– ) |
| *CLE* | F. Bücheler–E. Lommatzsch, *Carmina Latina Epigraphica* (Leipzig, 1897–1930). ( = *Anth. Lat.* Pars II) |
| *CRF* | O. Ribbeck, *Comicorum Romanorum Fragmenta*, 3rd. ed. (Leipzig, 1897) |
| *CSEL* | *Corpus Scriptorum Ecclesiasticorum Latinorum* (Vienna, 1866– ) |
| *CVA* | *Corpus Vasorum Antiquorum* (Paris & elsewhere, 1925– ) |
| Christ–Schmid– Stählin | W. von Christ, *Geschichte der griechischen Literatur*, rev. W. Schmid and O. Stählin (Munich, 1920–1924) 6th ed. (Cf. Schmid–Stählin) |
| *DTC* | A. W. Pickard-Cambridge, *Dithyramb, tragedy and comedy.* 2nd ed., rev. T. B. L. Webster (Oxford, 1962) |
| *DFA* | A. W. Pickard-Cambridge, *The dramatic festivals of Athens.* 2nd ed., rev. J. Gould–D. M. Lewis (Oxford, 1968) |

| | |
|---|---|
| DK | H. Diels–W. Kranz, *Die Fragmente der Vorsokratiker*. 6th ed. (Berlin, 1951) |
| *EGF* | G. Kinkel, *Epicorum Graecorum Fragmenta* (Leipzig, 1877) |
| *FGrH* | F. Jacoby, *Fragmente der griechischen Historiker* (Berlin, 1923– ) |
| *FHG* | C. Müller, *Fragmenta Historicorum Graecorum* (Berlin, 1841–70) |
| *FPL* | W. Morel, *Fragmenta Poetarum Latinorum* (Leipzig, 1927) |
| *FPR* | E. Baehrens, *Fragmenta Poetarum Romanorum* (Leipzig, 1886) |
| *FYAT* | (ed.) M. Platnauer, *Fifty years (and twelve) of classical scholarship* (Oxford, 1968) |
| *GLK* | H. Keil, *Grammatici Latini* (Leipzig, 1855–1923) |
| *GLP* | D. L. Page, *Greek Literary Papyri* (Cambridge, Mass. & London, 1942– ) |
| Gow–Page, *Hell. Ep.* | A. S. F. Gow–D. L. Page, *The Greek Anthology: Hellenistic Epigrams* (Cambridge, 1965) |
| Gow–Page, *Garland* | A. S. F. Gow–D. L. Page, *The Greek Anthology: The Garland of Philip* (Cambridge, 1968) |
| Guthrie | W. K. C. Guthrie, *A History of Greek Philosophy* (Cambridge, 1965–81) |
| *HRR* | H. Peter, *Historicorum Romanorum reliquiae* (Leipzig, 1906–14) |
| HS | J. B. Hofmann, *Lateinische Syntax und Stilistik*, rev. A. Szantyr (Munich, 1965) |
| *IEG* | M. L. West, *Iambi et Elegi Graeci* (Oxford, 1971–2) |
| *IG* | *Inscriptiones Graecae* (Berlin, 1873– ) |
| *ILS* | H. Dessau, *Inscriptiones Latinae Selectae* (Berlin, 1892–1916) |
| KG | R. Kühner–B. Gerth, *Ausführliche Grammatik der griechischen Sprache: Satzlehre*. 4th ed. (Hannover, 1955) |
| KS | R. Kühner–C. Stegmann, *Ausführliche Grammatik der lateinischen sprache: Satzlehre*. 3rd ed., rev. A. Thierfelder (Hannover, 1955) |
| Leo, *Gesch.* | F. Leo, *Geschichte der romischen Literatur*. I *Die archaische Literatur* (all pubd) (Berlin, 1913; repr. Darmstadt, 1967, w. *Die römische Poesie in der sullanischen Zeit*) |
| Lesky | A. Lesky, *A History of Greek Literature*, tr. J. Willis–C. de Heer (London, 1966) |
| Lesky, *TDH* | A. Lesky, *Die tragische Dichtung der Hellenen*, 3rd ed. (Göttingen, 1972) |
| LSJ | Liddell–Scott–Jones, *Greek–English Lexicon*, 9th ed. (Oxford, 1925–40) |
| Loeb | Loeb Classical Library (Cambridge, Mass. & London) |
| *MGH* | *Monumenta Germaniae Historica* (Berlin, 1877–91) |
| *OCD²* | *Oxford Classical Dictionary*, 2nd ed. (Oxford, 1970) |

| | |
|---|---|
| OCT | Scriptorum Classicorum Bibliotheca Oxoniensis (Oxford) |
| Paravia | Corpus Scriptorum Latinorum Paravianum (Turin) |
| PIR | E. Klebs–H. Dessau, *Prosopographia Imperii Romani Saeculi I, II, III* (Berlin, 1897–8), 2nd ed. E. Groag–A. Stein (Berlin & Leipzig, 1933– ) |
| PL | J.-P. Migne, *Patrologiae cursus completus* Series Latina (Paris, 1844– ) |
| PLF | E. Lobel–D. Page, *Poetarum Lesbiorum Fragmenta* (Oxford, 1963) |
| PLM | E. Baehrens, *Poetae Latini Minores* (Leipzig, 1879–83), rev. F. Vollmer (incomplete) (1911–35) |
| PLRE | A. H. M. Jones–J. R. Martindale–J. Morris, *The prosopography of the later Roman Empire* (Cambridge, 1971– ) |
| PMG | D. L. Page, *Poetae Melici Graeci* (Oxford, 1962) |
| PPF | H. Diels, *Poetarum Philosophorum Graecorum Fragmenta* (Berlin, 1901) |
| Pfeiffer | R. Pfeiffer, *A history of classical scholarship* (Oxford, 1968) |
| Powell | J. U. Powell, *Collectanea Alexandrina* (Oxford, 1925) |
| Powell–Barber | J. U. Powell–E. A. Barber, *New chapters in the history of Greek Literature* (Oxford, 1921), 2nd ser. (1929), 3rd ser. (Powell alone) (1933) |
| Preller–Robert | L. Preller, *Griechische Mythologie*, 4th ed., rev. C. Robert (Berlin, 1894) |
| RAC | *Reallexicon für Antike und Christentum* (Stuttgart, 1941– ) |
| RE | A. Pauly–G. Wissowa–W. Kroll, *Real-Encyclopädie der klassischen Altertumswissenschaft* (Stuttgart, 1893– ) |
| ROL | E. H. Warmington, *Remains of old Latin* (Cambridge, Mass. & London, 1935–40) |
| Roscher | W. H. Roscher, *Ausführliches Lexicon der griechischen und römischen Mythologie* (Leipzig, 1884– ) |
| SEG | *Supplementum Epigraphicum Graecum* (Leyden, 1923–71; Alphen aan den Rijn, 1979– ) |
| SVF | H. von Arnim, *Stoicorum Veterum Fragmenta* (Leipzig, 1903– ) |
| Snell | B. Snell, *Tragicorum Graecorum Fragmenta* (Göttingen, 1971– ) |
| Schanz–Hosius | M. Schanz–C. Hosius, *Geschichte der römischen Literatur* (Munich, 1914–1935) |
| Schmid–Stählin | W. Schmid–O. Stählin, *Geschichte der griechischen Literatur* (Munich, 1929–1948) |
| Spengel | L. Spengel, *Rhetores Graeci* (1853–6); I ii rev. C. Hammer (Leipzig, 1894) |
| Teuffel | W. S. Teuffel, *Geschichte der römischen Literatur* (Leipzig & Berlin, 1913–1920) |

| | |
|---|---|
| *TGF* | A. Nauck, *Tragicorum Graecorum Fragmenta*, 2nd ed. (Leipzig, 1889) |
| *TLL* | *Thesaurus Linguae Latinae* (Leipzig, 1900– ) |
| *TRF* | O. Ribbeck, *Tragicorum Romanorum Fragmenta*, 3rd ed. (Leipzig, 1897) |
| Walz | C. Walz, *Rhetores Graeci* (Stuttgart, 1832–6) |
| Williams, *TORP* | G. Williams, *Tradition and originality in Roman Poetry* (Oxford, 1968) |

# WORKS CITED IN THE TEXT

Allen, W. S. (1973). *Accent and rhythm: prosodic features of Latin and Greek*. Cambridge.

Arnheim, M. T. W. (1972). *The senatorial aristocracy in the later Roman Empire*. Oxford.

Blakeney, E. H. (1933). *Ausonius. The Mosella*. London.

Cameron, A. (1970). *Claudian: poetry and propaganda at the court of Honorius*. Oxford.

D'Alton, J. F. (1931). *Roman literary theory and criticism*. London.

Enmann, H. (1884). *Eine verlorene Geschichte der römischen Kaiser und das Buch De viris illustribus urbis Romae*. Philologus Suppl. IV 337–501.

Fraenkel, E. (1964). *Kleine Beiträge zur klassischen Philologie*. 2 vols. Rome.

Kroll, W. (1926). (ed.). *Historia Alexandri Magni (Pseudo-Callisthenes)* I: *Recensio vetusta*. Berlin.

Magie, D. (1921–32). (ed.). *The Historiae Augustae*. 3 vols. London & Cambridge, Mass.

Matthews, J. (1975). *Western aristocracies and Imperial court*. Oxford.

Mohrmann, C. (1961). *Études sur le latin des Chrétiens* II: *Latin chrétien et médiéval*. Rome.

Momigliano, A. (1962). (ed.). *The conflict between Paganism and Christianity in the fourth century*. Oxford.

(1969). 'Il trapasso fra storiografia antica e storiografia medievale', *Rivista storica italiana* 81: 286–303.

Nettleship, H. (1890). 'Literary criticism in Latin antiquity', *Journal of Philology* 18: 225–70.

Pichon, R. (1906). *Les derniers écrivains profanes*. Paris.

Platnauer, M. (1922). (ed.). *Claudian*. 2 vols. Loeb. London and Cambridge, Mass.

Wirszubski, C. (1950). *Libertas as a political idea at Rome during the late Republic and early Principate*. Cambridge.

# INDEX

*Main references are distinguished by figures in bold type. References to the Appendix (which should normally be consulted for basic details of authors' lives and works, and for bibliographies) are given in italic figures.*

# INDEX